The Complete Guide to
Writing & Publishing
Your First E-Book

Insider Secrets You Need to Know to Become a Successful Author

Martha Maeda

MAY   2015

THE COMPLETE GUIDE TO WRITING & PUBLISHING YOUR FIRST E-BOOK: INSIDER SECRETS YOU NEED TO KNOW TO BECOME A SUCCESSFUL AUTHOR

Copyright © 2015 Atlantic Publishing Group, Inc.
1405 SW 6th Avenue • Ocala, Florida 34471 • Phone 800-814-1132 • Fax 352-622-1875
Website: www.atlantic-pub.com • E-mail: sales@atlantic-pub.com
SAN Number: 268-1250

Library of Congress Cataloging-in-Publication Data

Maeda, Martha, 1953-
  The complete guide to writing & publishing your first e-book : insider secrets you need to know to become a successful author / by Martha Maeda.
    pages cm
  Includes bibliographical references and index.
  ISBN-13: 978-1-60138-608-3 (alk. paper)
  ISBN-10: 1-60138-608-7 (alk. paper)
  1. Self-publishing--United States. 2. Electronic publishing--United States. 3. Electronic books--Marketing. 4. Authorship--Marketing. I. Title.
  Z285.5.M34 2012
  070.5'73--dc23
                                    2012018169

Printed in the United States

Printed on Recycled Paper

A few years back we lost our beloved pet dog Bear, who was not only our best and dearest friend but also the "Vice President of Sunshine" here at Atlantic Publishing. He did not receive a salary but worked tirelessly 24 hours a day to please his parents.

Bear was a rescue dog who turned around and showered myself, my wife, Sherri, his grandparents Jean, Bob, and Nancy, and every person and animal he met (well, maybe not rabbits) with friendship and love. He made a lot of people smile every day.

We wanted you to know a portion of the profits of this book will be donated in Bear's memory to local animal shelters, parks, conservation organizations, and other individuals and nonprofit organizations in need of assistance.

– Douglas & Sherri Brown

PS: We have since adopted two more rescue dogs: first Scout, and the following year, Ginger. They were both mixed golden retrievers who needed a home.

Want to help animals and the world? Here are a dozen easy suggestions you and your family can implement today:

- *Adopt and rescue a pet from a local shelter.*
- *Support local and no-kill animal shelters.*
- *Plant a tree to honor someone you love.*
- *Be a developer — put up some birdhouses.*
- *Buy live, potted Christmas trees and replant them.*
- *Make sure you spend time with your animals each day.*
- *Save natural resources by recycling and buying recycled products.*
- *Drink tap water, or filter your own water at home.*
- *Whenever possible, limit your use of or do not use pesticides.*
- *If you eat seafood, make sustainable choices.*
- *Support your local farmers market.*
- *Get outside. Visit a park, volunteer, walk your dog, or ride your bike.*

Five years ago, Atlantic Publishing signed the Green Press Initiative. These guidelines promote environmentally friendly practices, such as using recycled stock and vegetable-based inks, avoiding waste, choosing energy-efficient resources, and promoting a no-pulping policy. We now use 100-percent recycled stock on all our books. The results: in one year, switching to post-consumer recycled stock saved 24 mature trees, 5,000 gallons of water, the equivalent of the total energy used for one home in a year, and the equivalent of the greenhouse gases from one car driven for a year.

Disclaimer

The material in this book is provided for informational purposes and as a general guide to writing an e-book only. Basic definitions of laws and instructions are provided according to their status at the time of printing; be sure to check for changes or updates in laws and publishing instructions. This book should not substitute professional advice for the publishing of your e-book.

Author Dedication

Dedicated to everyone who has an imagination,
a story to tell, and a desire to share it with the world.

Table of Contents

Chapter 4: Preparing to Publish Your E-book ... 75

Chapter 5: Working with Graphics in E-books 91

Chapter 6: An Introduction to E-Book Formats 101

Introduction

Every historical trend has a moment when it is poised to take off. For e-book publishing, that moment is now. E-books have been in the news so often over the past three years, it is difficult to keep up with the latest developments — almost every day there is an announcement about the newest e-reader or the latest e-book. In March 2011, the Association of American Publishers reported that in January of that year, monthly e-book sales had surpassed sales of hardcover books for the first time. In May 2011, Amazon reported that its sales of e-books officially had surpassed its combined sales of hardcover and paperback print books. In 2010, sales of e-books in the United States jumped 164 percent over the previous year to $441 million. By 2013, e-books brought in $1.3 billion in revenue. April 2014, Association of American Publishers reported that e-books now account for 27% of all adult trade sales.

A recent report by Forrester Research reported that the e-book market was now a $1 billion industry and predicted that e-book sales will reach $2.81 billion by 2015, when 29.4 million Americans will own dedicated e-reading devices. A report released by the UK-based research firm, Juniper, predicted that e-book sales will reach $9.7 billion worldwide in 2016.

The rapid rise in popularity of e-books is due to the enthusiasm with which booksellers and technology manufacturers are promoting e-reader technology and the speed with which large numbers of e-books are being made available for sale. E-readers, which retail for prices ranging from less than $100 to $600, represent a new product with a large potential market — everyone who can read. They are impressive and affordable gifts for any friend or relative who loves books.

In January 2014, many e-book authors noted a sudden and dramatic jump in their sales. Though the reasons for this are not fully understood, analysts believe it was partly due to large numbers of e-readers and e-book gift cards being given as Christmas presents in December 2013. The increasing popularity of tablets, such as iPad, also is driving e-book sales.

Readers and book lovers of all ages have embraced e-books and are reshaping the way books are marketed and sold. Children enjoy book apps, software programs that bring classic children's books to life with music, animations, and interactive games. Book lovers like the prestige and convenience of carrying entire libraries in their pockets and the satisfaction of being able to read, within minutes, obscure and out-of-print books by interesting authors. Millions of readers take delight in discovering new talent, recommending books to each other, and posting their reviews and opinions. Authors have discovered that e-books can be published as works in progress, to be modified, updated, and extended whenever it suits them.

Self-published e-books have created an arena where self-published authors can flourish and excel. Major e-booksellers like Amazon and Barnes & Noble display indies (books by independent authors) alongside e-books produced by traditional publishing houses, and indie e-book publisher/retailers, such as Smashwords, have built thriving online communities of writers and loyal fans. Internet searches, blogs, and social media allow authors, sitting at their computers in home offices, to promote their books to an international audience of millions of potential readers. Readers actively participate in reviewing, rating, and recommending e-books to other readers.

Are you ready to become part of the e-book phenomenon? If you have a manuscript ready to publish as an e-book or an idea for an e-book, this book will guide you through the process of editing and polishing your work, formatting it, and uploading it for sale on the Internet. Learn about your options for e-publishing and about how you can promote your book through online booksellers, social media, and paid advertising. Through these chapters, you will gain an understanding of the business aspect of e-publishing and develop a plan for a series of future e-books. You will learn to evaluate your market and produce e-books that will sell. Throughout the book, news excerpts and case studies provide real-life examples of successful e-authors and present interesting points of view.

By the time you finish reading this book, you will be well on your way to a career as an e-author. Every writer has a unique approach and unique circumstances. Make the most of your talents and abilities and achieve success on your own terms by publishing a successful e-book.

CHAPTER 1

When he entered the room, Fred knew he wouldn't be there long. He surveyed his surroundings and immediately decided he wouldn't find what he was looking for. It was dingy, a mess, and quite bitterly cold. And not just the temperature. The room itself was frigid. Its aura gave him the feeling he wasn't alone, and the other inhabitants, unseen spectres of another time, clearly didn't want him there.

But Fred had a job to do, as unseemly as it was. He had to find the redhead before the spirits grabbed hold of her. This was what he was hired to do, and he never let down a client.

"Hey Red," he called out, not expecting an answer, and of course he didn't get one.

"What do you want?" came a reply, though the sound of the voice clearly wasn't the object of his search.

"If you're looking for the deadbeat who was last in that room, she skipped town sticking me with three months' rent.

"If I pay up can I get some info on her?" Fred asked.

"That's quite a bill. You sure you're prepared to pay it?"

The question took Fred by surprise. How did this stranger know he himself had little more than a hundred bucks to his name? But that didn't matter now. He just had to convince the woman that he was a player and could meet her demands. Otherwise he had no hope of finding Red. And that wasn't an option.

◀ **PREVIOUS**   **NEXT** ▶

Why E-Publish?

One after another, writers are proclaiming their independence from traditional publishing publicly and declaring that e-books are the way to go. No more query letters, contracts, book-signing tours, and shipping and distribution costs, they announce. No more waiting to be offered a book deal and no more being relegated to a back shelf while your publisher promotes someone else's blockbuster. No more middlemen taking big chunks of the profit from your book sales.

The prospect is alluring — a worldwide audience of potential readers, unrestricted by physical location, able to buy your book with the click of a mouse. When someone buys your book, you receive up to 70 percent of the sales price and as much as 100 percent if you sell the book from your own website. E-publishing is almost free if you have some basic computer skills, compared with the money spent to produce copies of a self-published print book. Some self-published e-book authors are selling hundreds of their books every month and making a respectable income.

Although all these things are true, e-publishing is not as simple as it seems. In order to sell your e-book, you must make people aware of it and convince them to pay money to read it. This requires hard work and a certain amount of skill. To succeed as an e-author, you need a good understanding of the e-publishing business.

A Brief History of E-Publishing

The marketing and sales of e-book readers fueled the rise of e-books to prominence in just three years, between December 2007 and December 2010. Electronic files of books had been available to read on computers and the Internet for almost two decades, but the era of the e-book began with the debut of convenient e-reading devices that could be carried around and read on commuter trains or at the beach, just like paper books. Several book retailers and electronics manufacturers were quick to capitalize on the market. Amazon and Barnes & Noble realized they could profit twice, first by selling their customers e-readers, then by selling them hundreds of affordable e-books. During the same period, the rapid evolution of the self-publishing industry added millions of new titles to the market, all produced and marketed by the authors themselves, and many of these were made available as e-books.

E-Books in the Headlines

Stephen King first well-known writer to publish an e-book

Stephen King set off a media frenzy in March 2000 when he became the first well-known writer to release a book exclusively as an e-book. First-day downloads of *Riding the Bullet* surpassed first-day sales of all his previous paper best sellers. Scribner, an imprint of Simon & Schuster®, together with Softlock, Inc., a digital rights management company, released the book. Avid fans downloaded more than 400,000 copies of the book that first day. Some waited hours for the download, and the encryption caused many computers to crash. The book sold for $2.50. More than 500,000 copies were downloaded, but Softlock reported that many readers were unwilling to pay and that only 10 percent of these downloads were paid for. Amazon.com and Barnes & Noble ended up giving away many free copies.

Intrigued by the success of *Riding the Bullet*, King set another precedent that year by self-publishing another novella, *The Plant*, as an e-book. He released it on his website and suggested readers pay $1 for the first installment. He promised to release the rest of the book if 75 percent of the downloaders paid. By 4 p.m. on the day of release, more than 40,000 copies of *The Plant* had been downloaded.

The first e-readers

The earliest e-readers were ahead of their time. NuvoMedia released the first e-reader, the Rocket eBook, in 1998. The 22-ounce handheld device held about ten books and allowed the reader to underline text, set bookmarks, and make notes in the margins. It could connect to the Internet through a computer to download books. Soon afterwards, SoftBook Press, a venture by Simon & Schuster and Random House, launched a SoftBook Reader that connected directly to the Internet with a built-in connection. The EveryBook Reader, launched in 1999, could dial into the EveryBook Store and download books, magazines, and sheet music. Librius offered digital copies of thousands of books through its Millennium eBook, released the same year. In the fall of 2000, and again in late 2002, RCA's Gemstar, which had purchased Nuvomedia and Softbook Press, launched black-and-white and color versions of its Gemstar eBook, the REB 1100 and the REB 1200.

Sales of these early e-book readers fell far short of expectations, partly because of their high prices. The price of the Rocket eBook was $200; Softbook sold for $300 plus a $300 subscription to its bookstore,; and RCA's REB 1200 retailed for $699. The selection of electronic books available to read on these expensive devices was limited. (In 1999, Nuvo's library consisted of only 2,000 books.) Readers were unable to download the latest best sellers or find books on specialized topics. Wireless coverage was irregular, and downloading books from the Internet took time and persistence. Within a few years, most of these manufacturers stopped producing e-readers and withdrew from the market.

Launch of the Amazon Kindle

When Amazon launched its Kindle e-book reader in the fall of 2007, the circumstances were dramatically different. Amazon was positioned as the world's largest online bookseller as well as a powerful online retailer of electronics. Cell phone and wireless coverage reached most areas of the United States and Canada, which made it possible for a device to connect to the Internet from urban and many rural locations. People were accustomed to reading, listening to music, and watching movies on laptop computers.

The release of the first Kindle coincided with the start of the Christmas shopping season, and Amazon generated excitement months in advance through its website and a well-planned advertising campaign targeting millions of existing customers. The first edition of Amazon's Kindle, released on November 19, 2007, for a price of $399, sold out in five and a half hours (some sources say it was six). Kindles were back-ordered, and the stock was not replenished until April 2008. Amazon offered a selection of 80,000 books, including many *New York Times*® Best Sellers for $9.99, along with magazines and newspapers, available for download in minutes through a free wireless service.

Kindle e-readers sold out again early in December 2008, and in February 2009, Amazon released its second version of Kindle, replaced later that year by an international version incorporating 3G wireless. At the end of 2010 Amazon announced that it had sold 115 e-books for every 100 hardcover paper books that year, and that the Kindle 3 had surpassed the final Harry Potter novel to become the best-selling item in Amazon's history. In September 2013, Amazon released its third generation Kindle Fire HDX and forecasters estimate sales to be $11 million in 2014.

More e-readers

In 2009, Barnes & Noble launched its own e-reader, NOOK®, placing displays prominently in the front of every retail store and training its staff to encourage customers to buy them. Sales of the NOOK line of e-readers from October through December 2013 holiday season were $88 million.

Kindle and NOOK dominate in the U.S. because Amazon, the largest book retailer in the world, and Barnes & Noble, the largest book retailer in the U.S., market them. A variety of other e-readers, including Kobo™ eReader, PocketBook, iriver Story, and Samsung, are sold in bookstores, electronics stores, and large retailers. Consumers also read e-books using e-reader software on computers, on tablet devices such as iPads and Android™, and on cell phones.

Each successive generation of eReaders gets better and faster and has more features than the last, including touch-screen interfaces, 3G-wireless connections, improved backgrounds and colors, and larger memory drive. E-Reader manufacturers are vying to develop new technologies that will attract more buyers and inspire those who already own eReaders to trade in their older models for new ones. Since 2014, Amazon has six different versions of Kindle, just in time for another Christmas gift-giving season. In competition, Barnes & Noble just released NOOK GlowLight, featuring the product prominently in its retail stores. With this kind of impetus pushing sales of eReaders worldwide, the market for e-books is expanding rapidly. According to Pew Research Internet Project, the percentage of adults who read an e-book within the past year has risen to 28 percent, a 5 percent increase since 2012. Although only 4 percent of adults are e-book only readers, sales increase every year as shown in this chart:

	U.S. E-book Sales	Percentage of U.S. Book Market
2002	$2.1	0.05%
2006	$25.2	0.5%
2007	Launch of Amazon Kindle e-reader	
2008	$78.0	0.6%
2009	$169.5	3.2%

	U.S. E-book Sales	**Percentage of U.S. Book Market**
2010	$441.3	8.3%
2011	$1,700.0	18.6%

In 2010, e-book sales increased 164.4 percent over the previous year. In 2011, sales of e-books rose by 117 percent.

Publishers' e-book revenues were up 117.3 percent in 2011, and December e-book sales were 72 percent higher than the previous year.

E-Books and Paper Books

E-book Sales Growth, 2008 - 2012 (in millions)

Year	2008	2009	2010	2011	2012
Sales	$64.00	$291.0	$869.1	$2,109.0	$3,042.0
% chg	--	354.0%	198.0%	142.0%	44.0%

E-book Unit Growth, 2008 - 2012 (in millions)

Year	2008	2009	2010	2011	2012
Units	10.0	36.1	125.0	320.0	457.0
% chg	--	260.0%	247.00%	156.00%	43.0%

Though e-books are relatively new to some readers, certain trends already are emerging. While e-books keep growing, hardcover and trade paperback formats continued to hold steady in 2012, according to the Association of American Publishers. The indication is that e-books are stimulating interest in owning and reading books in general."

E-books require an initial investment to write, edit, design, and format them, but once an e-book is published, the cost of distribution is almost negligible. Hard copies do not have to be printed and shipped to bookstores that place them on the shelves and later ship back unsold copies to be redistributed or destroyed. They are immediately available to anyone with an Internet connection, anywhere in the world.

Unlike print books, e-books do not go out of print and disappear from the bookstore shelves. Your e-book remains available for readers to buy until you decide to take it off the market. Any new books you publish are likely to increase interest in your earlier releases and generate more sales.

E-book sales are driven by marketing and advertising, just like sales of paper books. Publicity of every kind is important, but some of the strategies are different. The physical location of the author or of book retailers is no longer a factor. Instead of sitting at a table and signing books in a bookstore, the author of an e-book might offer special benefits such as free chapters or discounts to fans who interact through a website, blog, or Twitter. An e-book can be tied in directly to an author's online presence by being linked to an email, a book review, or an interview.

E-books are ideal impulse buys. They sell more easily than hard copies because of their low prices (often $2.99) and because they are available to read in seconds. It is doubtful that e-book buyers ever read all the books they download, but their intentions are good. People sit at their leisure with e-readers, browsing through lists of fascinating titles and thinking, "Ooh, I want to read that!" and, "Oh, I should read that…" They do not have to overcome the distractions of walking to the front of a bookstore, waiting in line, pulling out a wallet, and parting with $20 or $30.

E-books confer many benefits for self-publishers. You do not need to invest hundreds of dollars in printing hard copies, shipping, storing, packaging, or fulfilling orders. There are no returns of unsold books from bookstores, and it costs nothing to send out free promotional copies. Though the price of an e-book is lower than the price of a paperback book or a hardback, the author gets as much as 70 percent, which often amounts to more than the royalties from the sale of a hard copy. An e-book can be sold directly through a link in an email, from a blog, a website, a newsletter, or an online bookseller. E-book conversion services charge as little as $100 to format a book for electronic publishing, and an author familiar with HTML or Microsoft Word can do his or her own formatting. Many print-on-demand (POD) printers of paper books offer an e-book option as part of their packages, which makes it easy for a self-publisher to sell both print versions and e-books.

E-books offer many opportunities to enrich the reading experience, and publishers quickly are developing enhancements. Audio and visual add-ins, such as video clips, music, photo galleries, and narrators reading text can be added to an e-book. Readers can look up a definition in a dictionary, access notes and background information, and leave comments on social media with a touch of the screen. Most e-readers allow the reader to type or write notes, which are organized and easily accessible. The entire text can be searched in seconds for a particular word or phrase. Some have text-to-speech software that reads a book aloud to you.

E-readers also offer physical enhancements, like the ability to enlarge the text for easier reading, and a backlit screen that can be read without any other light source. A reader can customize the appearance of the text in an e-reading device to his or her own preferences.

Electronic books can be updated quickly and easily, so a reference book or textbook always has the latest information. Many important scientific papers are published in journals months after a new discovery has been documented; this information could be made available to readers electronically in just a few days. Owners of medical guides, technical manuals, text books, and travel books can access frequent updates and always have access to the most current knowledge of a subject. A subscription to an e-magazine entitles you to search back issues electronically and reread interesting articles whenever you want to.

Are E-Books "Greener" than Print Books?

The debate is raging — are e-books better for the environment and for society than print books? A number of studies have attempted to compare the environmental impact of print books and e-readers, but a definite conclusion has not been reached. Several factors must be considered, including the resources used to manufacture and transport both print books and e-readers, the amount of carbon emissions produced during each process, and the quantity and type of waste discarded.

- According to a report by CleanTech Group, the U.S. book and newspaper industries combined require the harvesting of 125 million trees per year.

- The amount of carbon emissions produced during the manufacture and transportation of an average paperback book (its carbon footprint) is about 10 pounds. More than 80 percent of this is produced while manufacturing the paper the book is made of.

- Between 25 and 36 percent of all books are returned to the publisher unsold, and many of these are destroyed. Shipping them back to the publisher produces even more carbon emissions.

- Energy is required and carbon emissions are produced during the manufacture of e-readers, too. Apple® reports that the carbon footprint of an iPad equals the carbon footprint of 32 paperback books. Amazon and Barnes & Noble have not released information about the manufacture of the Kindle or NOOK to allow comparison. Some experts estimate that the carbon footprint plus water and mineral consumption of an e-reading device equals that of 40 to 50 paperback books.

- The manufacture of electronic devices requires the use of small quantities of rare minerals mined in countries like Democratic Republic of Congo, where the profits from selling them help to finance civil wars. Electronic devices also contain toxic materials such as lead, mercury, and cadmium, which must eventually be disposed of. Obsolete electronics end up in landfills or are sometimes shipped illegally to Asia where the villagers who dismantle them, and their children, are exposed to these toxins.

The conclusion: The longer you own your e-reader and the more books you read with it, the greener it is.

The downside of e-books

E-books have undeniable limitations, many of them linked to the technology used to transmit and read them. No matter how widespread e-book usage becomes, it never can replace paper books completely.

- Paper books that are hundreds of years old still can be read if they have been stored properly. It is doubtful that an e-reader will last more than a decade or two at most, and its memory may degrade in a few years. Electronic components deteriorate more quickly than quality paper and cardboard.

- Current e-readers require a variety of file formats; in a decade or so, newer technologies might not be able to access them all. You may not be able to pass your favorite books on to your children or reread a novel you bought 15 years ago.

- No technology is required to read a paper book. E-readers are still expensive enough to put them beyond the reach of a large segment of the world's population. People living in poverty might be increasingly sidelined as more information and literature is published electronically.

- Electronic technology requires access to a power source such as a battery or electric current. Power failures or a breakdown of Internet networks caused by a natural disaster, political uprising, or cyberterrorism could make e-readers unusable.

- If an e-reader is lost, stolen, or dropped in a swimming pool, its owner can lose hundreds of dollars' worth of e-books in an instant. Some e-book sellers, including Amazon, maintain your library on their servers so you can upload it onto a new device, but if you have bought books from several sources, this could be a tedious process.

- New technologies become obsolete quickly; soon we will be swapping out e-readers just like we do cell phones. The more people purchase e-readers, the more old e-readers will end up in landfills or gathering dust in a box in the garage.

- Current e-book prices are competitively low, but consumers of e-books are at the mercy of e-book publishers and retailers. If prices of e-books start to rise beyond what readers are willing to pay, few alternatives exist apart from borrowing e-books from a library or renting them for short periods. Libraries lend e-books using DRM software that prevents copying and disables the file after three weeks if you do not renew the book. There are now several companies that allow students to rent e-textbooks for a semester instead of buying them.

- When you purchase an e-book, you do not own it the same way you own a paper book. Unlike paper books, e-books cannot be re-sold as used books, shared, or loaned to a friend. Some e-book publishers are now offering the option to loan an e-book to someone else but often restrict the number of times it can be borrowed. You cannot recoup some of the cost of a new e-book by selling it when you are finished with it, as many students do with textbooks.

- Many e-books are copy-protected with some kind of digital rights management (DRM), and each e-book retailer accomplishes this using a different method. Books sold, or offered free, by one retailer cannot be read with another retailer's e-reader. For example, a Kindle book cannot be read on a NOOK. You can get around this, including using Calibre® (**http://calibre-ebook.com**), a free software program that converts one format to another, or the Amazon service that converts books to Kindle, but you must invest extra time and effort before you can read a particular book.

- E-book readers are not convenient for some purposes. Cookbooks have been difficult to adapt as e-books because the smaller screen does not allow the reader to see the whole recipe conveniently at a glance. A cook with sticky hands cannot scroll down or turn pages on an e-reader. Books with photographs such as art books and coffee table books can be e-published, but the reader experience is not the same. Though interactive enhancements promise exciting possibilities for children's books, e-readers cannot reproduce the tactile features that appeal to small children, such as cutouts and textures. Flipping back and forth on an e-reader can be frustrating in situations in which a researcher needs to consult several books simultaneously.

- There is no universal format for e-books — each e-reader has a proprietary format for the books sold from its e-bookstore. When you download books from a different supplier, you have to convert the files so you can read them on your device. This complicates the organization and storage of your e-book library.

- The page numbers of e-books change in different e-reader formats, which makes it difficult to cite references. When citing an e-book, you must give the type of e-reader as well as the page number. In March 2011, Amazon began adding "location numbers" to Kindle books that show the page number of the physical book.

Though digital files provide the same content, they do not necessarily provide the same experience as reading a paper book. Nothing can replace the physical experience of browsing through the shelves of a bookstore or library surrounded by thousands of books, taking down whatever book catches your eye and cracking it open to skim a random page. Though e-book retailers attempt to emulate these actions with free chapters, sampling, and "look inside" features, not everyone wants his or her reading experience to be dictated by the conventions of an e-reader or a website.

- For centuries, book ownership has been a symbol of prestige and an expression of personality and individuality. Collectors value paper books for their historical significance and appearance. Books displayed in a home hint at the values and interests of the person living there. The titles in an e-book reader cannot be displayed on a shelf for visitors to admire. E-books will make paper first editions more valuable over time.

E-Books in the Headlines

E-Textbooks Cut College Costs

Collegeboard.org reports that U.S. college students pay an average of $1,200 per year for their textbooks. The Student Public Interest Research Groups report that over the past decade, textbook prices have increased three times the rate of inflation.

A single textbook for some subjects can cost more than $200, and publishers constantly are releasing new editions that make used books obsolete. One solution being promoted is free and open-source e-textbooks. Flat World Knowledge, Inc. (**www.flatworldknowledge.com**), the largest publisher of free and open-source college textbooks, offers almost 100 free e-textbooks online. Professors can edit and adapt textbooks for their classes. Students can read the texts online free or purchase affordable print and digital formats, including e-books, audio books, PDF downloads, interactive study aids, and black-and-white or full-color printed textbooks. E-textbooks are also available for elementary, middle, and high school courses.

CourseSmart® (**www.coursesmart.com**), a digital textbook company started by five major textbook publishers, offers more than 20,000 digital titles students can read on any device that has an Internet browser. CK12 (**www.ck12.org/flexbook**) has open-source textbooks for students of all ages. The California Open Source Textbook Project (COSTP) (**www.opensourcetext.org**), which began in 2001 as a public/private collaboration, seeks to address the high cost and consistent shortage of textbooks in public schools and claims its program could reduce costs by 80 percent.

Inkling® (**www.inkling.com**) offers a free iPad app for its interactive textbooks, which it says are 40 percent cheaper than their print versions. Many college bookstores now sell e-textbooks alongside their paper counterparts. Some high schools and colleges are pioneering paperless textbooks. Northwest Missouri State University, which for a long time has kept students' expenses down by buying textbooks and renting them to its students for a low, flat fee, has begun buying e-textbooks instead. Some students still express re-luctance to switch from paper to electronic textbooks, but administrators believe the interactive features of e-textbooks will improve the learning experience.

Google reported that online searches for "Kindle textbooks" and "NOOK textbooks" were up 60 percent over the previous year. Searches for "iPad textbooks" were up 40 percent. Students may not have bought e-textbooks, but they were certainly looking for them. Used textbooks and textbook rentals are still cheaper than buying e-textbooks, and some critics are concerned that, because e-textbooks cannot be re-sold or loaned, they could trap students into paying higher prices for some books.

The Business of E-Publishing

Writing a good book, formatting it, and making it available online is only part of successful e-publishing. The other part is marketing and sales. Best-selling authors of self-published e-books succeed because they work hard to publicize and promote their books. Marketing involves a variety of activities, from researching your audience before you decide on a topic to designing an eye-catching cover and building your "platform" — the public reputation that will attract potential buyers. *Chapters 11 and 12 talk about ways to market your e-book.*

Traditional publishing houses

While commentators are making dire predictions that e-books will under-mine the conventional publishing business, traditional publishing houses have been leading the way in exploiting the sales potential of e-books. Nearly every book-publishing contract includes a clause concerning ownership of the rights to publish the manuscript as an e-book. E-book versions of new releases are prepared alongside the hardcover and paperback print versions, though they sometimes are released a few days or weeks after the hardcover hits the bookstores. E-book launches are timed to coincide with author appearances in the media or with events that will generate public interest in their topics.

E-books are a boon to traditional publishing houses, just as they are to self-published authors. A new release e-book by a best-selling author can be priced around $20, just a few dollars less than the hardcover, because fans are anxious to read it as soon as it comes out — yet producing the e-book version costs the publisher only a small fraction of the cost of printing, distributing, and shipping the print books.

Publishing houses have the resources to produce high quality e-books. Manuscripts have gone through regular editing and proofreading processes. Staffs of professionals are employed to design and format the e-books and add the enhancements they believe will appeal to readers. Publishers use their established distribution channels and negotiate with major book retailers such as Amazon and Barnes & Noble to distribute a new book in multiple formats at once. Little additional marketing is needed to sell e-book versions of new print releases. The same publicity that sells print books sells e-books, too.

E-books also have opened new avenues of sales for traditional publishing houses. Readers who like one e-book by a particular author are inclined to buy the author's entire backlist (all the books previously published by that author). A publishing house cannot afford to print runs of older books and keep them in stock on the chance a few interested customers might ask for them, but it easily can provide e-book versions of its entire catalog. Bookstores cannot carry large numbers of out-of-print books on their shelves. E-book retail sites offer hundreds of specialized and out-of-print books. Many books, including most fiction published before 1900, are now in the public domain. A publishing house can format and repackage classics for sale as e-books when it would not be practical or cost-effective to produce print versions.

Many reference books such as encyclopedias and directories (including *Writer's Market*) are now sold as online subscriptions or regularly updated e-books. Instead of replacing massive volumes when they become obsolete every year or two, readers can access the latest facts by downloading or updating e-books. Publishers can refresh the content constantly as circumstances change and new information becomes available.

E-books can be written and produced in a short time because they do not have to go through the physical process of printing and distribution. This allows publishing houses to commission and release e-books on topics of current interest within days of an event.

E-Books in the Headlines

Real-Time E-Books about the 2012 Presidential Election

In June 2011, Random House and Politico® announced they would partner to publish four 20,000 to 30,000 word e-books on the 2012 election, written by Politico's chief White House correspondent, Mike Allen, and Evan Thomas, a political reporter for *Newsweek*® and *Time*®. The first book was published in November 2011 in time for the Christmas season.

> The publishers were confident that the American public would want to read accounts of behind-the-scenes political maneuvering while it was actually happening instead of waiting until after the election.
>
> Penguin-Random House reported that in 2013 e-books accounted for about 20% of their pro forma revenue. Simon & Shuster's e-book sales were up 20% in 2013. During the same period, sales of print books continued to drop but at a slower rate than in 2011-2012.

Self-published e-books

There are as many ways to market an e-book as there are e-book authors. E-books are sold through online book retailers using the same advertising techniques as print books sold online, as well as strategies unique to e-books. Authors who have a readership for their print books have little difficulty attracting buyers for their e-books. Some e-authors establish themselves as bloggers and sell books as extensions of their blogs. An expert in a particular field, such as a financial guru, can sell e-books from his or her website. Professors create customized e-textbooks for their students. An author with a brick-and-mortar business, such as selling solar panels, might write and sell do-it-yourself e-books to customers from the business website. Websites for indie (independent, self-published) authors, like indie music sites, attract a broad community of fans looking for something new and interesting to read. Online communities of e-book readers have sprung up around specific genres. Though some authors sell their e-books independently, the most effective way to reach large numbers of potential buyers is by attracting as much attention as possible on the websites of established online book retailers such as Amazon and Barnes & Noble.

The success of a self-published e-book is measured according to the author's expectations. Some e-book authors simply want to express themselves and are content if their books are bought and read by a small circle of acquaintances. They may be more interested in educating the public, spreading ideas, or supporting a cause than in making money. Others aim to make a substantial income by reaching a wide market and building a base of fans who will want to buy their future books.

CASE STUDY: COZY MYSTERY WRITER SUCCESSFUL IN KINDLE PUBLISHING

Gayle Trent
www.gayletrent.com

Gayle Trent is a cozy mystery author living in Southwest Virginia. She writes two cozy mystery series, the Daphne Martin Cake Decorating mystery series, and the Marcy Singer Embroidery mystery series.

I have always loved writing. My first book was published in 1999 after much trial and error. I love reading mysteries of all sorts, but the cozy mystery is my favorite genre to write because it is just so much fun. The characters are quirky, and they get involved in some crazy situations.

I have written e-books in the past, but my book that has been most successful in e-publishing is *Murder Takes the Cake*. It has done very well on the Kindle. *Murder Takes the Cake*'s publisher, Bell Bridge Books, participated in a Kindle promotion wherein publishers gave free Kindle downloads of their books for a limited time. *Murder Takes the Cake* was very successful; in fact, it became a Kindle best seller. I was skeptical of the book's success, as it was free. Who would not want a free book? However, I saw the trade paperback version of *Murder Take the Cake* rise to an Amazon Sales Rank of 5,814 in books and No. 31 in Mystery Series on Jan. 2, 2010. *Dead Pan*, the sequel to *Murder Takes the Cake*, is also doing well in the Kindle Store — although not free.

As for self-publishing, investigate all your options, and remember that marketing is key. If you are not willing to market and publicize your book, and if you are not sure who your audience is, then do not self-publish.

Your "business plan" for your e-book will help define the extent of your financial investment in publishing and marketing it. It is possible to spend little and do most of the work of writing, editing, formatting, designing, and publicizing yourself. However, if you are confident you can produce a top seller, you might invest thousands of dollars for editing and book design services, a professional cover design, e-book conversion, paid book reviews, and Internet ads. Always think about how many copies you will have to sell to cover the cost of producing and marketing it. Professional services are not free, but you might be able to cut corners by enlisting the help of friends or fellow writers to edit your book and offering your services to an artist in exchange for a professional cover.

Your first e-book probably will not be your last. Readers will be interested in purchasing your future books. While you are working on your first book, plan how you can expand on its success with additional books. In the traditional publishing world, an author could spend months in limbo trying to sell a manuscript to a publishing house, and then wait another two years before the book appears in bookstores. A self-published book can be released as soon as you are finished preparing it, which leaves you free to plunge into your next endeavor.

E-Books in the Headlines

Joe Konrath, E-Book Legend

Joe Konrath (**www.jakonrath.com**), author of the Jack Daniels mystery series and one of the top-selling authors in Amazon's Kindle store, described in a famous blog post in January 2011 (**http://jakon rath.blogspot.com/2011/01/time-investment.html**) how hard he worked to promote his first three print novels, *Whisky Sour, Bloody Mary*, and *Rusty Nail*. In 2005, he spent $4,000 and 80 hours of labor to send signed *Bloody Mary* drink coasters and a sales brochure to 6,500 libraries. In 2009, for another book, *Afraid,* he appeared on 100 blogs in 30 days and toured

200 bookstores. To promote *Rusty Nail,* he drove almost 11,500 miles, visited 504 bookstores, and signed 4,066 books. In four years, *Rusty Nail* earned $42,000 in royalties. In January 2011, he made the same amount in one month selling his self-published e-books through Kindle, Smashwords, Createspace®, and Barnes & Noble while doing no promotion at all. In his blog post, he announced that he would no longer be doing promotional tours and would be devoting all of his time to writing more books.

A growing number of self-published authors are selling several hundred e-books per month. Besides bringing in a respectable income, self-published e-books with substantial sales figures attract the interest of conventional publishing houses. A successful e-book author who already has demonstrated that his or her books will sell can command higher advances from traditional publishers than a first-time author.

E-Books in the Headlines

John Locke

In June 2011, John Locke, author of a series of e-thrillers including *Vegas Moon, Wish List,* and *A Girl Like You,* became the first self-published author to sell more than one million Kindle e-books on Amazon. In September 2011, he signed a deal with Simon & Schuster to distribute eight of his books in print, retaining his status as a self-published author and publishing the books through his John Locke imprint.

You can learn how he did it by downloading *How I Sold 1 Million eBooks in 5 Months* for $4.99. His first secret: pricing his books at $0.99 to attract buyers. Because Amazon pays a 35 percent royalty for e-books priced under $2.99, which translates into earnings of $0.35 per book or about $350,000 for his one million sales.

Chapter 2

Writing an E-Book that Will Sell

E-books literally sell themselves. A reader browsing online sees an interesting title or cover, clicks on it to learn more, reads the book copy and some sample text, and then decides to buy. A reader who likes your e-book will then look to see what other books you have written or recommend your book to a friend or colleague. Your title, cover image, and introductory chapter are crucial. Spare no effort to make your book a success.

Like any commercial product sold online, your e-book should be designed carefully to appeal to potential buyers. The subject matter, cover design, sample excerpts of the text, book reviews, and publicity all influence the buyer's decision to purchase and read an e-book. Readers who are satisfied with their first experiences will want to buy more e-books by the same author and more e-books of the same genre.

Your first e-book is the foundation for your career as an e-author. A sloppy, amateurish, poorly formatted e-book could deter readers from ever looking at one of your books again. Every reader you convince to buy your e-book is one more success. You never know which one of your readers will write a great review, recommend the book to dozens of friends, or introduce it to a talk-show host or a mainstream publisher. Do not risk losing a single potential fan because of carelessness, lack of visibility, overpricing, or bad cover design.

If you already have finished writing your manuscript, take time to edit and polish it to perfection before launching it into cyberspace. If your e-book is still in the planning stages, evaluate your potential market and study your competition. Form a clear idea of what you hope to accomplish, and then find out what you must do to achieve your goal.

Choosing a Subject

You might know what you want to write about, but the way you approach your subject matter can make the difference between a mediocre e-book and a top seller. Visit bookstores and websites of online book retailers to see what books are being released about similar topics. Look at the titles on best-seller lists to see what readers are buying. Even if dozens of books have been written on your topic, you can write with a new twist, specialize in one particular aspect, or produce the definitive book on the subject.

Write what you know

Anything you have first-hand knowledge of can become a topic for a non-fiction book or provide rich and detailed background for a story. Make a list of everything you know. Write down your academic degrees and professional certifications, education, training, work experience, hobbies, sports, volunteer work, personal relationships — anything you can think of. Are you a grandfather, a mother, a best friend, or a child of an alcoholic? Are you a veteran? A Little League® coach? An accountant? A massage therapist? Do you love to bake cookies or play fantasy football? Perhaps you have been a Sunday school teacher for 20 years, spend your winters in Alaska training sled dogs, or are a regular contestant in barbecue cook-offs. You might have built your house yourself out of cordwood or breed canaries as a hobby. Your home might be a family farm in Utah or a tiny apartment in Manhattan. Maybe you operate a successful Internet business from your home or commute an hour every day to your job in a financial firm.

Think about how you can share your expertise or teach someone else to do the same thing you have done. Write about one or more problems you have encountered and how you resolved them. Write a book that would have helped you at some point in your life or your career. Tell everyone what you wish you had known when you started out or what you realized because of your efforts. Thousands of other people in similar situations could benefit from your experience or at least enjoy reading about it.

Draw from your personal experience

Take a moment to examine your life. In a journal or notebook, write your answers to questions such as, "What am I doing right now?" "What are my goals?" "Where have I been?" "What are my priorities?" "What am I trying to achieve?" "What is my biggest problem right now?" Others probably are asking themselves similar questions, and a book exploring your personal odyssey might resonate. Tony Robbins, the well-known self-help guru and author of *Unlimited Power* and *Awakening the Giant Within*, likes to recount how, at the lowest point in his life, he vowed to change his attitude and succeeded in transforming himself.

A story about overcoming personal obstacles or dealing with a personal crisis makes compelling reading. A number of best-selling e-books have originated with blogs in which the authors talked about their emotional reactions to a life event, such as the birth of a child or a divorce.

Who do you know? Your experiences as a relative or friend of a well-known person might make an interesting story. You also could recount his or her story from your point of view. You might have a neighbor or friend who is an expert in some field and is willing to collaborate on a book.

You could write a book about how a personal difficulty affected your life and how you dealt with it — for example, how you survived being laid off and found a new job, or how you learned to manage diabetes while playing professional baseball. Your child might have been bullied at school, or you might be caring for a parent with Alzheimer's disease. A book can contain facts, but your thoughts and feelings make it unique.

Remember that people do not like to be reminded of sad situations, such as the terminal illness of a child, even when they are facing similar circumstances themselves. If you want to write about something like surviving the death of a loved one or living with a disability, write from a positive, inspirational viewpoint.

Read, read, read

You cannot write without reading. Go to bookstores and libraries, and browse through books and magazines about your topic. Read new releases and best sellers to see what is popular and what the latest trends are. When you find a book that interests you, take note of the publisher. Look on that publisher's website to see what books are scheduled for release next season. Bookstores often have free catalogs of upcoming releases — pick one up and look through it.

Watch talk shows, listen to the public radio, and read newspapers to see what the public is thinking and talking about. Do not follow a trend too closely because by the time your e-book is released, a new trend will have taken hold of the public imagination. Instead, come up with a new take on a popular concept, such as "green" living or stay-at-home dads, and anticipate the next trend.

Look up topics on websites of online booksellers such as Amazon.com, Barnes & Noble, and Alibris™. Read the book reviews and sample excerpts. Notice the other books recommended alongside your choices.

When you have identified a topic you would like to write about, look at the books and magazines in that category or section of the bookstore and ask yourself what is missing. For example, most of the travel books for South

America might be for affluent travelers, with little or no information for young people on a budget. Low-calorie cookbooks might be lacking Asian recipes. Articles on historical events might overlook the role of women.

Set up Google "Alerts" to send you relevant information

Go to Google.com and select "Alerts" under "Specialized Search." (Get there by clicking "more" and then "even more" on the menu at the top of the Google screen.) Enter relevant keywords for your topic. Google will send you email alerts every time a new article is published about your topic.

Know your genre

Genre is a set of criteria for a category of fiction or nonfiction. Knowing a book's genre helps a potential reader know what to expect emotionally, structurally, and intellectually. Genre creates a set of expectations, and your job as the writer is to know what those expectations are and deliver them to the reader.

Understanding your genre helps you market your e-book effectively to readers. Just like physical bookstores, online book retailers categorize books by genre and use genre names as keywords so they appear in Internet search results. Most online book retail sites recommend additional books based on genre.

If you are writing fiction, immerse yourself in your genre by reading books from other authors, following blogs, and joining writers' groups. Some genres, such as science fiction, fantasy adventure, and paranormal romance, have developed large online communities of fans in which you can participate to help promote your e-books. *Appendix A contains a list of genres with their descriptions.*

E-Books in the Headlines

Amanda Hocking

In 2009, when she was 24, Amanda Hocking decided to take writing seriously and treat it as a job. At first, she wrote young adult romance novels, but after some research she discovered that stories with paranormal elements were popular and began writing about vampires and trolls. Frustrated when publishers rejected her novels, she began self-publishing them as e-books in March 2010. Her sales began to take off in June 2010, when she began sending free copies of her books to bloggers to review. By the end of 2010, she had sold 164,000 books. In January 2011, during the sudden burst of e-book sales that followed Christmas 2010, she sold more than 450,000 copies of her nine books. By March 2011, she had sold more than one million e-books on multiple platforms. She attributes her success to low prices — she priced her books according to what she would be willing to pay for an e-book, at either $0.99 or $2.99, and to stories that keep readers coming back for more, as well as aggressive self-promotion on Facebook, Twitter, and her blog (**http://amandahocking.blogspot.com**).

> In March 2011, Hocking announced a $2 million contract with St. Martin's Press to publish four books. On her blog, she explained, "I *only* want to be a writer. I do not want to spend 40 hours a week handling e-mails, formatting covers, finding editors, etc. Right now, being me is a full-time corporation."

Understanding Your Market

Large publishers continually analyze sales figures, survey bookstore customers to see how they react to new releases, and monitor industry news and statistics. A carefully orchestrated advertising campaign designed to motivate as many people as possible to buy the book accompanies each new release. When that publicity dies down, publishers strategize to continue sales by promoting the book through book clubs, talk shows, media interviews, and price discounts. Be equally aware of the market for your e-book — who is likely to buy it, where and how they buy e-books, and what kind of media they enjoy. You will need this information to develop an effective publishing and marketing plan for your book.

How large is the potential audience for your e-book? If your topic is interesting only to members of your family or to a small, highly specialized community, do not expect to sell thousands of downloads. Browse the sales ranks of similar books on the market and review the best-seller lists in your genre to get an idea of how many potential readers exist for your book. *Publishers Weekly*® magazine online (**www.publishersweekly.com**) provides best-seller lists and columns on "Retail Sales" and "Trends and Topics" you might find helpful. *The New York Times'* Book Review section (**www.nytimes.com/pages/books**) also lists best sellers by category. The website NovelRank (**www.novelrank.com**) allows you to track Amazon.com sales rank history by book URL, author or title and compare similar books by genre or title.

Writing a book for a highly specialized market is not necessarily a disadvantage if you have an effective way to communicate with your audience. A book on local history could be promoted on local news and information websites, or a technical book could be promoted on the website of a professional association. If your goal is to become a best-selling author by publishing e-books, however, write on topics that appeal to a broad audience.

Romance Fiction is the Top-Selling Genre

According to the Romance Writers of America, the estimated annual total sales of the romance fiction genre generated $1.4 billion in 2014, surpassing other genres such as mystery, science fiction/fantasy, and religious/inspirational. Romance fiction has become a large share of the consumer market for published books. It's the top-selling genre in adult fiction and makes up 13 percent of all adult fiction. Some of the bestselling subgenres include category, contemporary, paranormal and historical romance.

About 84 percent of women purchase romance fiction, which has gone down from its 90.5 percent readership a few years ago; men now make up 16 percent of romance readership. According to the Romance Writers of America, romance-fiction readership is aged between 30 to 54 years and mainly resides in the south.

About 36 percent of romance readers subscribe to an eBook service that recommends romance eBooks for purchase (by matching interest and providing discounts etc.). The average eBook pricing is $6, too. Romance fiction is a booming genre that has become very successful in eBook market. You should consider producing romance novels because there is a great likelihood that you will make a successful profit, especially in eBook sales.

The audience for e-books is not the same as the audience for print books. A report released in August 2013 by the Pew Internet Project concluded that approximately 26 percent of adults owned e-readers, up 8 percent from the year before. About 34 percent of U.S. adults reported owning a tablet computer such as an iPad, Samsung Galaxy, or Motorola Xoom™. Some of this ownership overlapped; 3 percent of U.S. adults owned both an e-reader and a tablet. The same survey revealed that owners of e-readers were most likely Hispanic adults, adults younger than age 65, college graduates, and those living in households with incomes of at least $75,000. Also, parents were more likely than non-parents to own e-readers. Five percent of college graduates owned e-readers.

E-reader ownership is increasing most rapidly in the age group between 18 and 49. These numbers show that many people still do not own e-readers and that people buying e-readers tend to be younger, wealthier, and better educated than the general public. A report by Forrester Research reported that only about 14 percent of all general consumer fiction and nonfiction books sold were e-books. Considering these statistics, a book on estate planning in retirement might not be as good a candidate for e-publishing as an edgy, chick-lit novella or a self-help book for young professionals. Some interested readers are out there for any topic, but some topics will attract many more readers.

Make Your E-Book Available in Print

After you publish your e-book, consider making it available in print for the large percentage of potential readers who still do not own or use e-reading devices or who would like to carry around a paper version of your e-book. You can upload your manuscript to Lulu.com® or Amazon's Createspace (**www.createspace.com**) free. It will be made available for sale through online retail outlets, and you will receive a percentage of each sale, just as you do for e-books. Before uploading your manuscript, you must format it using word-processing software and insert chapter and section breaks, page headers, page numbers, title pages, blank pages between chapters, a table of contents, and an index. The document then must be converted to a PDF file. The exact specifications for formatting your manuscript can be found on the Createspace website. You can upload your book cover image or design a cover using one of the publisher's free templates. If this is too complicated or time-consuming for you, most POD publishers offer formatting services for a fee, or you can pay a freelancer to prepare the manuscript for you. The print version will have a separate ISBN number. Your print book will be offered for sale alongside your e-book by online bookstores, and you can put a link for purchasing the print version on your author website. The publishing company processes orders and takes care of shipping the print books.

Writing for E-Readers

A book of any size can be published as an e-book. Massive tomes like *War and Peace* and *Atlas Shrugged* can be downloaded and read on an e-reader just as easily as a short book like *Jonathan Livingston Seagull.* If you like to read in bed, an e-reader is lighter and easier to hold than several hundred pages of paperback.

E-readers have given rise to new genres and new products. Because e-books do not have to be printed and shipped to bookstores in a particular form, they allow authors and publishers to experiment with different ways of presenting written material. Many authors serialize books and sell them one chapter at a time for $0.99 each. The word count of a printed book ranges from 50,000 to 115,000 words; some e-books are as short as 10,000 words. Novelettes (7,500 to 17,499 words) and novellas (17,500 to 40,000) are ideal reading for commuters, travelers, and readers who want a brief escape from reality. Writing shorter books also allows authors to experiment and move on to new concepts without investing in a full-length novel. Authors can alter and republish their books at will, offer readers a choice of endings, and publish prequels, sequels, and supplementary material. Readers do not object to paying $0.99 to $4 for an unconventional book or one by an author they know little about.

Some authors sell their work as subscriptions to "magazines" or serialized publications released at regular intervals. Bloggers and journalists compile their posts and articles into short e-books. Many authors offer free excerpts and even whole books to attract readers.

E-Books in the Headlines

Newspapers and Magazines Publish Their Own E-Books

Magazines and newspapers have begun publishing compilations of their articles and previously published material as e-books. Because they employ journalists and writers, it costs them little to edit and prepare the e-books.

- *Vanity Fair* published a collection of 20 articles about the phone-hacking scandal at Rupert Murdoch's News Corporation for $3.99.

- *The New Yorker* released a commemorative e-book for the anniversary of 9/11 for $7.99.

- An e-book published by *The New York Times*, *Open Secrets*, reached #19 on *The New York Times* E-book Nonfiction Best Seller List.

- The Huffington Post began publishing e-books in September 2011.

- Other news entities publishing e-books include ABC News, *The Boston Globe*, and Politico.

E-reader limitations

Reading from an e-reader is not the same as reading from a printed page. The text on the e-reader screen can be enlarged (or shrunk), which means the reader is not always looking at an entire page. Many people download and read e-books on their cell phones, which have even smaller screens. E-readers often are used in situations where the reader is frequently interrupted or has a short attention span, such as on a bus or commuter train, in a restaurant, or a crowded outdoor area.

When you are writing specifically for an e-reader, follow these guidelines:

- Write in short paragraphs of three or four sentences. A long paragraph that fills up the entire screen may discourage the reader. Short paragraphs can be taken in at a glance and read in a few seconds.

- Use lists instead of paragraphs or strung-out sentences to present information whenever appropriate. Make the items in the lists short and easy to read.

- "Chunk" your information — break it up into short segments conveying individual concepts and ideas.

- Divide the book into chapters and sub-chapters to help readers find their way around.

- Most e-books are formatted in HTML. If you plan to do your own formatting, avoid including illustrations and charts unless you are an experienced HTML editor. It requires patience and skill to format charts and tables. For books that rely on diagrams and illustrations, using a conversion service will guarantee a professional-looking book.

- Most owners of e-readers are familiar with the writing conventions used in blogs, texting, and social media, and for some genres such as chick-lit, it is acceptable to use abbreviations, short sentences, and symbols in place of words.

Perfecting Your Writing

If you are serious about selling your book, you must be serious about the quality of your writing. Good writing brings together many elements: imagination and creativity, style, a consistent point of view, knowledge of the subject matter, clever plot structure, appropriate vocabulary, and correct grammar and sentence construction.

Good writing skills are not acquired overnight, and some people never master the technical aspects of grammar and sentence structure. Perhaps you have a captivating story to tell but lack a rich vocabulary and the ability to write well-crafted sentences. You might have a good idea and excellent writing skills, but lack the knowledge and authority to produce a marketable manuscript. Do not let obstacles like these stand in your way. Improve your writing by participating in a writing workshop or creative writing classes. Hire a professional editor to rework your manuscript, or partner with a co-writer or a ghostwriter.

Using checklists to improve your book

A good way to self-edit your manuscript is to use a checklist, a questionnaire that helps you review your work for important qualities. As you ask yourself whether you have accomplished each item on a checklist, you become aware of weaknesses and areas where you can make improvements. A checklist enables you to take a step away from your manuscript and see it through a potential reader's eyes.

Fiction

Story checklists are helpful for self-diagnosing problem areas of your fiction manuscript. Many checklist books exist solely for this purpose, such as Elizabeth Lyons' *Manuscript Makeover: Revision Techniques No Fiction Writer Can Afford To Ignore* and *Self-Editing for Fiction Writers* by Renni Browne and Dave King.

A well-written work of fiction is characterized by:

- A powerful, distinctive "voice"
- Unique story line
- Original, compelling, well-crafted sentences
- Interesting characters
- Dialogue that reveals character and subtext
- Narrative that evokes images
- An intriguing and immediate opening hook that contains action, conflict, and crisis

The following story checklist will help you pinpoint weak areas to revise your fiction manuscript:

- Rewrite sentences that begin with the words "There" or "It."
- Revise sentences written in passive voice.
- Check that the tone is consistent for your story and genre.
- Ensure all dialogue and speeches advance the story and reveal plot and character.
- Make sure your prose is fluent and varied in rhythm.

To make sure the plot of your fiction novel is as perfect as your grammar, ask yourself the following questions:

- Does each of my characters have a distinctive voice?
- Is the antagonist as complex as the protagonist?

- Is the main character's opponent as strong or stronger?

- Do I open the story as late as possible?

- Does the opening grab the reader and compel him or her to continue reading?

- Is there enough conflict flowing through the entire book to hold a reader's attention?

- Is there a compelling reason for readers to connect with the hero and follow him on his journey?

- Does the plot unfold naturally?

- Have I crafted a key relationship for the protagonist whom readers can relate to and root for?

- Is the theme consistent throughout the narrative?

- Does the writing evoke an emotional response for the reader?

- Is too much exposition delivered in one section?

- Does each chapter end with a cliffhanger?

- Does each scene contain conflict or tension?

- Have I successfully conveyed the main character's transformation?

- Are my descriptions vibrant and detailed?

- Does the ending pack a punch and leave the reader satisfied?

The Top Five Qualities that Make a Fiction Manuscript Mediocre

1. The writing is too predictable — there are no surprises or twists.

2. The author does too much "telling" and not enough "showing" — stating how a character feels instead of showing it through action.

3. The characters are not interesting or worth caring about — there is nothing compelling to engage the reader.

4. The protagonist does not undergo a transformation — the main character is the same person at the end of the story as he or she was at the beginning of the story.

5. The author does not have a distinct voice — the style and diction of the narrative filtered through the author that creates a sense of uniqueness.

Nonfiction

When going over your nonfiction book, review the purpose for which the book was written. Confirm that the manuscript fulfills that purpose and meets the expectations aroused by the book title, introduction, and book copy on the back cover.

A good nonfiction work has these qualities:

- A strong narrative element
- A structure that flows logically and leads the reader to a specific goal
- Writing that delivers help to solve a problem or make one's life better

Follow the steps below to self-edit a nonfiction manuscript:

- Rewrite sentences that begin with the words "There" or "It."
- Revise sentences written in passive voice.
- Check that the tone is consistent throughout the book.
- Make sure your prose is fluent and varied in rhythm.
- Remove unnecessary words and phrases that are not essential to the meaning of a sentence.
- Avoid using superlatives (such as "great," "huge," "extremely," "terrific") or clichés ("and more") unless you have a good reason to use them.

- Make sure your verbs agree with the subject of the sentence (one ... is, some ... are) and that pronouns agree with the nouns they refer to. ("company...its," "people...their").

Ask yourself the following questions when you are critically evaluating your nonfiction book:

- Is the introduction compelling? Does it explain how the reader will benefit from my book and entice the reader to delve further into the book?

- Is the book well organized, with an outline and a clear progression from one topic to the next?

- Are headings, sidebars, numbering, chapter introductions, and title headings consistent throughout the book?

- Are there short, choppy sentences that could be combined to make a smoother, longer sentence?

- Are there long, awkward sentences that could be broken up into shorter segments and recombined?

- Is the meaning of each sentence clear?

- Does each paragraph have a topic sentence that is then developed further in the rest of the paragraph?

- Does the text flow smoothly from one idea to the next?

- Is the text broken up into short paragraphs, with lists, charts, diagrams, sidebars, and checklists to make it more interesting?

- Are all quotations properly cited?

- Have you checked all your facts with reliable sources? Is everything up-to-date, with reference to the most recent sources?

- Does the book accomplish its purpose?

- Does the conclusion recap the book with an inspiring message? Some readers will look at the conclusion before buying your book.

Editing and Proofreading

Writing and editing require different abilities. An imaginative writer might not be a good editor. Editors are language specialists, fanatical about grammar, spelling, sentence structure, and the correct use of punctuation. If you lack these skills, you will need help to edit your book. Even if you are a good editor, you will be so involved in your book that you might not spot mistakes and weaknesses.

A publishing company puts a manuscript through several rounds of professional editing and proofreading before it is published. The manuscript is checked carefully for typographical errors, spelling, spacing, punctuation, capitalization, sentence structure, syntax, word choice, tense, arrangement, overall clarity and flow. When you self-publish your book, you are responsible for making sure there are no errors. You may be in such a hurry to get your book on the market that you overlook mistakes, but this will make your book appear amateurish and unprofessional. After pouring so much effort into writing your book, it is worth investing some extra time and money to make it perfect.

You can find a professional freelance editor or proofreader through freelance websites, or by asking other writers for recommendations. The Editorial Freelancers Association (**www.the-efa.org**) provides a directory of qualified freelance editors and proofreaders and a standard rate chart. The three basic levels of editing are:

- Proofreading: A proofreader reviews your manuscript for spelling or grammatical errors, typographical errors, inconsistencies, and problems with page layout. Proofreaders' fees average between $25 and $35 per hour.

- Copyediting or line editing: Copyeditors and line editors read the text word for word and correct grammatical mistakes, typographical errors, and incorrect word usage. They also correct inconsistencies in style, alert you to unclear or problematic passages in the text, and note where you need to get permissions for copyrighted material. A line editor will make minor changes to improve readability and research the accuracy of facts. Basic copyediting costs $25 to $40 per hour, and line editors charge an average of $40 to $65 per hour.

- Developmental editing: A developmental editor makes suggestions about the content and organization of a book and might work with the author to develop a manuscript from an initial concept or draft. He or she may rewrite segments of the text to improve clarity, reorganize paragraphs and chapters, and recommend changes to the manuscript. Developmental editors' fees range from $50 to $80 per hour.

Editing software

The grammar and spell-check features in word processors will catch basic errors, but they will not pick up every mistake. Editing software programs catch disagreements in verb tenses, punctuation and abbreviation errors, misused words, and passive sentences. An editing program helps you learn how to improve your writing as well as pointing out mistakes and weaknesses in sentence structure.

Based on grammar books and style guides, Serenity Editor (**www.serenity-software.com**) can identify more than 200,000 common spelling errors, mechanical errors, usage mistakes, and stylistic misdemeanors. The software costs $55, but you can download a free 10-day trial. Grammar Expert Plus (**www.wintertree-software.com/app/gramxp/index.html**) costs $60 and offers a 30-day free trial.

Proofing your own manuscript

Ask friends, fellow writers, or family members to help you by proofreading sections of your book for typographical and grammatical errors. Another pair of eyes will see mistakes you have missed. Here are some techniques for proofreading your own manuscript:

- Take a break for several hours or days before going over your manuscript again. Your fresh eyes are likely to spot errors you missed before.

- Print a copy of the manuscript and trace each word with your finger. Some mistakes are more obvious when you see the book in print.

- Review your manuscript backwards from the end to the beginning, so you are proofing the words themselves rather than reading it.

- Read the manuscript aloud to catch missing or misspelled words and lapses in clarity.

- Print two copies and read one aloud, while a spouse or friend with a good knowledge of grammar and spelling follows along on the other copy.

E-Books in the Headlines

Borrowing of e-Books from Libraries continues to grow

OverDrive (**www.overdrive.com**), which provides digital distribution services for more than 30,000 libraries, school, and booksellers worldwide have experienced double digit growth since 2011. More than 1.6 billion book and title catalog pages were viewed on Overdrive's Virtual Branch library websites, up 130 percent from 2010. The OverDrive catalog for libraries now includes 2 million copyrighted e-book, audiobook, music, and video titles in 52 languages. Five million users downloaded the free OverDrive e-book and audiobook software, an increase of 84 percent over 2010. More than 11 million people now have installed this software. E-books also can be borrowed from libraries using a number of e-reading devices.

Becoming a Better Writer

Great authors never stop learning and improving on their writing. As you go on to create more e-books, seek out ways to improve your writing. Read books about writing and review well-known style guides like the *Chicago Manual of Style* (**www.chicagomanualofstyle.org**), *The Elements of Style* by William Strunk Jr. (**www.bartleby.com/141/index.html**), and the *Associated Press Stylebook* (**www.apstylebook.com**), available free through many libraries and universities.

Read books by other authors in genres similar to yours and learn from them. Read newspaper and magazine articles and literary classics to increase your vocabulary and improve your writing style.

Beta readers and critique partners

"Beta readers" are people who give you feedback on your manuscript while you are still working on it. Beta readers look for typos and grammatical errors, loose ends, passages that need to be clarified, and flaws and weaknesses in your manuscript.

A beta reader is anyone willing to read your book, including friends and family members. You also can find volunteer readers by joining writers' groups and participating in online writers' communities such as Absolute Write (**http://absolutewrite.com**) and Writers Beat (**www.writersbeat. com**), or virtual reader communities such as Library Thing (**www. librarything.com**) and Good Reads (**www.goodreads.com**). Get at least one objective opinion from a person who has professional knowledge of writing and publishing, and take his or her advice seriously.

Most people who volunteer to be beta readers enjoy reading books of a particular genre and encouraging emerging authors. Beta reading is most effective when you tell your reader what kind of feedback you want — a general opinion, proofreading, or a line-by-line critique — and give the reader a deadline. Some beta readers offer suggestions and correct errors.

However, do not hand your work in progress (WIP) over to a complete stranger without first learning something about him or her. A beta reader should want to support you in achieving your goals, and your relationship should be one of trust and mutual respect. It is unlikely that a beta reader would steal your work because it is copyrighted as soon as you write it, but if you feel uneasy, give him or her only one or two chapters to start with. Hold back on sending the rest of your manuscript until you are certain you can trust the person.

A critique partner is a fellow writer who comments on your work in exchange for your feedback on his or her writing. The ideal critique partner writes in a similar genre to yours, agrees with you on fundamental issues, and has the same or a higher level of experience writing professionally. Search for someone who has the qualities you need in a critique partner by joining local writers' groups and associations, networking at conferences, reading blogs and forums, and posting notices. Do not be shy about approaching fellow writers — the worst they can do is say "no." As with beta reading, critiquing works best when each partner clearly understands what is expected. Some critique partners sign informal contracts specifying how they will communicate (email, face-to-face meetings), how often they will exchange manuscript pages, and policies about turnaround time, deleting/returning material, and sharing emails with others.

Try out a potential critique partner by exchanging some trial pages before you commit yourself. The relationship between critique partners can be delicate because criticism is being exchanged, and not all comments are positive. A successful critique partnership often develops into a deeper professional relationship or a personal friendship.

More about Critique Partners

You can discover local critiquing partners via the Internet. Below are a few websites where you can reach out to other writers and benefit from productive critiquing sessions:

- For female writers, *Ladies Who Critique* is a great site for women to read each other's material and make impacting suggestions: **http://www.ladieswhocritique.com**

- On *Twitter*, you can reach out to a sea of writers and published authors. Send them a tweet or message and ask if they would be interested in critiquing. You never know what great feedback you'll get if you don't reach out on Twitter.

- *Sub It Club* is a great website to meet a critique partner and very easy to use: **http://subitclub.wordpress.com/2014/05/06/finding-critique-partners**

- Another great critique partner-finding website is *Write to Done*. This website not only offers great tips and advice for writing, but also provides potential critique partners: **http://writetodone.com/tag/critique-partners**

Writer critique groups comprise authors with an understanding of the writing craft. The goal of a writers' group is to help everyone involved become a better writer, so each member offers critiques of other members' manuscripts. You can find writers' groups in your community by inquiring at your local library and independent bookstores. You also can locate writers' groups online by using a search engine or exploring writing forums. For Writers (**www.forwriters.com**) offers a listing of writers' groups around the country.

Chapter 3

Copyrights and Legal Issues

Whether you are publishing your e-book as a commercial undertaking or because you want your voice to be heard, you have two important legal concerns. How are you going to prevent someone else from exploiting and profiting from your original, creative work? And how are you going to protect yourself from lawsuits accusing you of stealing someone else's work or causing some other type of financial loss? Writers, artists, and musicians are serious about protecting the creative work that earns them their livelihoods.

Publishing companies employ staffs of lawyers to handle contracts and legal challenges. As a self-publisher, you do not have a legal department to back you up. You are personally responsible for your book. Never assume that just because your book is small and obscure, or you sell only a few copies, no one is going to notice you have "borrowed" copyrighted material or made unsubstantiated allegations. Once your book is in the public arena, and you are selling it or using it to promote yourself, you can be held liable for its content. The best way to protect yourself is to be careful to get written permission for any copyrighted material you use, and make sure your information is factual.

Copyright

Copyright laws protect your legal ownership of original created work. According to the U.S. Copyright Office (**www.copyright.gov**), copyright is a form of legal protection granted by law for original works of authorship fixed in a tangible medium of expression. A copyright gives the owner the exclusive right to make copies, license, and otherwise exploit a literary, musical, or artistic work in printed, audio, or video form.

Copyright covers both published and unpublished works. You do not have to register a copyright to protect your work; it is under copyright protection the moment it is created and fixed in a tangible form that is perceptible either directly or with the aid of a machine or device. Tangible forms include books, manuscripts, sheet music, film, videotape, microfilm, electronic files, audio files, and recordings on cassettes, CDs, or vinyl disks. For example, you can "fix" an essay in a Word document or record it as an audio file, or both. If your work is prepared over time, the part of the work fixed on a particular date constitutes the created work as of that date.

Copyright registration is voluntary, but you will have to register if you wish to bring a lawsuit for infringement of a U.S. work. Register your book if you feel its contents might be taken and used for commercial purposes by someone else.

Copyright notice

A copyright notice informs your readers that your book is copyrighted material and sets out the conditions, if any, under which you will allow it to be used by someone else.

> The copyright notice is part of the book's front matter — the material that goes in the beginning of the book. Check the front matter in several print books to get an idea of how these are laid out.

The copyright notice should be placed just after the title page of your book: the symbol © (the letter C in a circle), or the word "copyright," followed by the author's name and the year the book was first published. Revised or derivative versions should have the year the revised version was first published.

Example: © 2015 Author Name

The copyright symbol, rather than the word "copyright," is necessary for international recognition and protects your work worldwide. In some e-readers, the copyright symbol appears as a question mark. To get around this, insert the copyright symbol as a graphic image instead of a text character.

The copyright is attributed to the owner of the work, which can be the author, publishing company, or the purchaser of the work.

In addition to this, you can put "All rights reserved" or a more detailed statement that no part of the book can be reproduced without written permission, along with contact information for obtaining that permission.

The copyright notice should appear on every copy of your book. Check to make sure it is there, and check any new versions of your book that you prepare for new formats or for publication in print.

What to put on your copyright page

- The word "copyright," the copyright symbol © (the letter "c" with a circle around it), and the copyright holder's name, which is usually the author or publisher.
- Trademark information (if any)
- Printer information (if the book has also been published in print)

- Publisher membership information
- The statement, "All rights reserved"
- Country where the book was printed or published
- Printer address (if applicable)
- CIP data (if the book is available in print)
- ISBNs,
- Cover and book design information, and attributions
- Edition number and dates
- Any other relevant publication, book, and copyright data

Unless your material is considered public domain, include the following paragraph:

> *All rights reserved. This book may not be reproduced in any form, in whole or in part (beyond that copying permitted by U.S. Copyright Law, Section 107, "fair use" in teaching or research, Section 108, certain library copying, or in published media by reviewers in limited excerpts), without written permission from the publisher.*

(Note: The publisher is you. Include an email address or contact information where requests for permission can be sent.)

Copyright registration

Copyright registration is not a condition of copyright protection. Registration is a legal formality intended to make a public record of the basic facts of a particular copyright. However, registration provides several legal advantages:

- Registration establishes a public record of the copyright claim.

- In the U.S., registration is necessary before you can file an infringement suit in court.

- If made before or within five years of publication, registration will establish prima-facie evidence in court of the validity of the copyright and of the facts stated in the certificate.

- If registration is made within three months after publication of the work or before an infringement of the work, you can claim statutory damages and attorney's fees if a court judges in your favor. Otherwise, you can claim only an award of actual damages and profits.

Registration may be made at any time within the life of the copyright.

An application for copyright registration contains three essential elements: a completed application form, a nonrefundable filing fee, and a nonreturnable deposit — that is, a copy or copies of the work being registered and "deposited" with the Copyright Office. A copyright registration is effective on the date the Copyright Office receives all required elements in acceptable form, regardless of how long it takes to process the application and mail the certificate of registration. The time needed to process applications varies depending on the amount of material the office is receiving and the method of application.

Register a claim with the Copyright Office within three months after the book's publication. Online registration through the electronic Copyright Office (eCO) (**www.copyright.gov**) is the preferred way to register basic claims for literary works. After you have paid the $55 online registration fee, you can upload your e-book. Follow the instructions on the U.S. Copyright Office website (**www.copyright.gov/eco/faq.html#eCO_2.2**).

You also can complete Form CO on your personal computer, print it out, and mail it along with a check or money order and two printed copies of your book (Word documents are fine; you do not have to go through the effort of formatting your e-book just for copyright purposes). Do not save your filled-out Form CO and reuse it for another book because it contains a unique barcode. The fee is $85 to submit Form CO by standard mail. You also can obtain the form from the Library of Congress website (**www. loc.gov/copyright/forms**). If you cannot access and print a Form CO on a computer, you can obtain a paper Form TX by mail from the U.S. Copyright Office.

Your copyright is in effect as soon as the registration form, payment, and copy of your e-book are received. Once your application is processed, the Copyright Office sends a copy of it stamped with a seal and signed by the registrar containing a date and registration number. Keep this for your records. Processing may take up to nine months or longer, as the number of annual applications processed by the office hovers around 600,000.

Copyright Infringement and Plagiarism

Copyright infringement and plagiarism are not necessarily the same. Plagiarism is representing someone else's words as your own without giving proper credit. It would not be copyright infringement to claim you wrote one of Shakespeare's sonnets because his works are too old to be under copyright. Plagiarism is not technically illegal except at schools and universities. However, you will lose credibility as an author, and no one will respect you or take your work seriously if you claim someone else's work as your own. On the other hand, even if you openly give another writer full credit, you are guilty of copyright infringement if you do not obtain written permission to use an excerpt in your book. Ignorance of copyright law is not an acceptable excuse in court. Always get written permission to use someone else's written words, photographs, or illustrations.

Ideas and facts cannot be copyrighted, only the words with which they are expressed. Do not repeat more than three significant words in a row as another person writes them. If you would like to use the words (more than one sentence) or images of another person, obtain his or her permission in writing.

Fair Use

Section 107 of the U.S. Copyright Law (title 17, U. S. Code) allows the "fair use" of copyrighted text for certain purposes, such as literary criticism, comment, news reporting, teaching, scholarship, and research. However, "fair use" is not clearly defined; no specific number of words, lines, or notes may be used safely without permission for these purposes. In a legal challenge, four factors are used to determine fair use:

- The purpose of the use and whether it is for commercial purposes
- The nature of the copyrighted work
- The percentage of the copyrighted work used
- The effect of the use on the commercial value of the copyrighted work

It is better to get written permission than to risk paying legal costs to defend yourself in court and possible damages if you lose.

Facts and systems cannot be copyrighted, either. A phrase or sentence spoken in a public setting can be re-quoted because it is a "fact" that the statement was made in public. An entire speech cannot be quoted in this manner, though. It is always safest to get permission to use quotes, unless the doctrine of fair use clearly applies — for example, a professor including quotes from an author in a lecture about that author's work.

Consider copyrights when you are selecting art and illustrations for your book, and be careful when using images found on the Internet. If you use original illustrations you or someone else created specifically for your book, and you have the creator's full permission to use the images, you are within rights. Ensure you credit the source properly within the book — that is, on the cover, title page, and copyright page. You automatically own the rights to anything you create. You also own the rights to anything created for you as a "work for hire." Be sure to get a signed agreement from the creator acknowledging he or she relinquishes all rights to the "work for hire."

Music and song lyrics

Most popular song lyrics are covered by copyright. In order to use even one line in your book legally, you might have to purchase an expensive license. Before you include lyrics in your book, check with a music licensing service such as LicenseMusicNow.com (**http://licensemusicnow.com**). Even hymns or folk songs could be under copyright protection. The same is true of audio recordings; never add music to an e-book or audio book without first obtaining a license or written permission to use it.

Images

Illustrations, drawings, maps, and photographs make a book more interesting. Be careful to get permission, however, for any images you include in your book. The safest option is to use original photos and illustrations that you create yourself or that someone creates specifically for your book. The person who creates an image automatically owns the rights. Make sure you have the creator's full permission to use the images. If you take photos of other people, get written consent to use their photos in your book.

You can find freelancers to create illustrations through websites such as Elance® (**www.elance.com**), Guru.com (**www.guru.com**), or Hireanillustrator.com (**www.hireanillustrator.com**).

Do not "borrow" pictures from the Internet. Old paintings might be in the public domain, but reproductions of them might not be. Many museums raise money by licensing images of paintings in their collections for use as posters and illustrations. Get written permission to use maps, charts, and illustrations, and follow instructions for citing the source.

A wealth of royalty-free images is available through various sites on the Internet. When you purchase a royalty-free image, you can use it as often as you like in your book, on posters and advertising copy, and on your website. Royalty-free images are sold on sites such as Thinkstock® (**www.thinkstockphotos.com**), Getty Images® (**www.gettyimages.com/Cre-**

ativeImages/RoyaltyFree), iStockphoto® (**www.istockphoto.com**), Time Tunnel (**www.timetunnel.com**), and Photos.com (**www.photos.com**).

Public domain images can be found on Creative Commons. To locate images on Creative Commons, visit **http://search.creativecommons.org**. Public domain images are free to use, but as mentioned above, it is always a good idea to get written permission from the creator. The disadvantage of royalty-free images is that they are available to anyone. You could find the same image in another e-book.

The use of a rights-managed image is sold exclusively to one buyer for a specified period. When that time has expired, you have to renew the license to continue using the image. Rights-managed images are available from companies such as Katzman Stock (**http://katzmanstock.com**), Illustration Works® (**www.illustrationworks.com**), and Mira (**http://library. mira.com**). Although you do not want to fill your book with rights-managed images, it might be worth paying for a striking image to use on your book cover.

Libel

Libel is the publication of an untrue statement that damages someone's reputation. For example, it would be libel to report incorrectly that an athlete is a drug addict because such a report could affect the athlete's career. In order to win a libel case in court, the claimant has to prove the damaging statement is untrue and that it was made with deliberate malice. No financial damages will be awarded unless the claimant can prove your statement was false, and people who bring libel suits lose more often than they win.

Even if you win in court, however, you must pay all your legal fees, which could amount to tens of thousands of dollars. If you lose a libel case, the damages awarded could be high. In some states, libel is a criminal as well as a civil offense, and you could end up serving a jail sentence in addition to paying financial compensation. In the U.S., under the First Amendment (freedom of speech) reporting about the lives and activities of public persons is not an invasion of privacy, but laws are different in other countries. Because the market for e-books is global, you risk being sued by someone outside the U.S.

If you are writing a book about living persons or their families, or about current events:

- Make sure your statements can be verified by several reliable sources.

- Limit yourself to commenting objectively on events without making damaging or unsupported insinuations.

- If you are stating your personal opinion, make that clear in your book.

- If a character in your fiction book is based on a living person, portray him or her in a way that is not clearly identifiable with the real person.

If your book is of a libelous nature, such as an exposé, a tell-all story, an in-depth analysis of a criminal case, or Wall Street scandal, and it might receive widespread attention, consider purchasing media liability insurance. You can find a list of companies offering this kind of insurance on the USC Annenberg Journalism Review website (**www.ojr.org/ojr/law/1077147945. php**). Media liability insurance costs several hundred dollars a year, but it could protect you from large financial losses.

Fact Checking

Unsubstantiated "facts" circulate easily on the Internet. While you are writing your e-book, avoid taking facts from blog posts or self-authored sites such as Wikipedia.com and Examiner.com. Use legitimate and reliable sources like major newspapers, government agencies, professional associations, scientific journals, and research companies. When you come across an interesting fact on a blog, trace it back to its original source. Always verify that you have the most recent information available.

Publishing houses employ fact-checkers that go over books and verify that dates, statistics, place names, locations, and other factual details are accurate. You could find yourself in an embarrassing situation if your book contains incorrect information. The credibility of your entire book is undermined, and conventional publishers or authorities in your field will not take you seriously. To save time, check facts as you go along. Learn to recognize factual material that needs to be verified, including the spelling of names and places, birth dates and places, the order of historical events, statistics, and financial figures. Take a few minutes to look up the information in an online reference or by typing the information in a search engine and finding news articles and research reports.

Bibliography, Footnotes, and Citations

A nonfiction book should include a bibliography at the end listing the sources from which you obtained information. Not only does a bibliography give well-deserved credit to other authors, it contributes to the credibility and professionalism of your book. It also provides readers who want to explore your topic more deeply with a valuable resource, which increases their respect and appreciation for you.

Include enough information in the bibliography about each source to allow readers to locate the information for themselves: author name(s), title of the article or book, publisher name, date of publication, and website address (if applicable). Various styles can be used for a bibliography, depending on its purpose. Be consistent — use the same style and arrangement for all your listings. For example, all author names should be listed in the same way.

Make the job easier by generating all your bibliography listings on a website such as EasyBib (**www.easybib.com**) or WorldCat® (**www.worldcat.org**). Copy and paste them onto a Microsoft Word or Open Office page, then highlight the whole page, and use the alphabetization feature to put them in alphabetical order with one mouse click.

Footnotes can be used to tell the reader where specific information came from or to give explanations and background information. Again, be consistent and use the same presentation style for all your footnotes. E-reading devices handle footnotes differently. Some require the reader to click on an asterisk, which opens a note from the back of the book in a new page. The reader then returns to the original page with a "Back" button. Others use pop-up boxes or plus signs that expand the footnote within the page itself. If you follow your e-publisher's instructions for formatting footnotes, they will appear as they should for a particular e-reader. Because opening up footnotes is a distraction for the reader, use them only where necessary. If you are quoting facts and figures repeatedly from the same source, it is better to create one note explaining where all the information came from instead of inserting a footnote for each occurrence of a fact.

Disclaimers

Some types of books, such as books giving medical or nutritional advice, instruction manuals, or financial guidance, could make you the target of a lawsuit if someone claims he or she was harmed following your advice. Add some legal protection by including a disclaimer at the front or back of the book — text stating you are not liable for personal injury to or damage to the property of someone who used your book. Look at other books in your genre to see if they include a disclaimer, and use similar legal language to create one for your book.

Chapter 4

Preparing to Publish Your E-book

W hen you are satisfied that your manuscript is ready for publication, it is time to plan how you are going to publish and market your e-book. You will need to select a title and design an appealing cover for your e-book. Your manuscript must be formatted for publication as an e-book. Finally, you must decide whether you are going to sell your book through a single bookstore, multiple retailers, or directly from your own website or blog. Each e-book retailer has a different format and a slightly different system for calculating and paying royalties. Every sales channel has its own means for promoting your e-book and grabbing the attention of potential readers.

What Are Your Options?

There are several ways to make your e-book available for sale:

Upload directly to a major e-book retailer

Upload your e-book directly to one of the major e-book retailers — for example, through Barnes & Noble's NOOK Press (**https://www.nookpress.com**) or Amazon's Kindle Direct Publishing (KDP) (**https://kdp.amazon.com**). You pay nothing to upload your book, and the retailer takes a cut of each sale. Your e-book appears on the retailer's website alongside books by well-known authors, and you can participate in the retailer's marketing initiatives, such as book ratings, reviews, and promotion alongside other books in the same genre. You can publish your e-book through more than one retailer. Each retailer offers various opportunities for promoting your book. *Learn more about publishing for the Kindle and the NOOK in Chapters 7 and 8.*

Through a free e-book conversion/retail site

E-book conversion/retail sites such as Smashwords (**www.smashwords.com**) and ScribD (**www.scribd.com**) allow you to upload and convert your manuscript free in exchange for a percentage of each sale. Follow their guidelines to format your manuscript, and upload it along with a cover image. Your book is made available for purchase on the retail site. Most of these sites distribute your e-book to Barnes & Noble, the Apple iBook store, and other outlets, and take a percentage of each of those sales as payment. Though you are paid slightly less per sale, a single upload gets your book into multiple retail outlets, and you do not have to spend time formatting and uploading it to each retailer individually.

Through an e-book conversion service

If you do not want to spend the time to format your manuscript, or if your book contains complex graphics or illustrations, you can pay for a professional e-book conversion service that will take your Word document, convert it to various e-book formats, and upload it to e-booksellers. A conversion service also can turn your book into an iPhone app or an e-book app — a small computer program that plays videos or allows database searches as part of the content. The current price for an e-book conversion starts at $100. You can find these services on the Internet by typing "e-book conversion" into a search engine. E-book conversion services often offer additional services for fees, such as marketing programs and paid ad campaigns. Many have their own online retail stores and writers' communities.

Shop carefully for an e-book conversion service. Like vanity presses, some overcharge for their services or try to talk you into purchasing add-ons, such as publicity and marketing campaigns of dubious value.

Tips for working with an e-book conversion service:

- Purchase only the services you need. The basic service is formatting your manuscript and converting it to one or more file formats. Some services accomplish this simply by formatting and uploading your document to Smashwords. Other services include proofreading and editing, cover design, and marketing activities, such as soliciting reviews. Because these marketing activities usually are automated, their value is questionable.

- Compare at least three conversion services before making your selection. Compare prices, payment policies, and services. Is the language used on the company's website professional? Does the company have an active user support forum or customer support that answers all your questions? Look at the books and authors published through each conversion service.

- Find out exactly what you are paying for. Some services use automated conversion software, while others offer professional formatting and a high-quality finished product.

- Make sure you are not relinquishing the rights to your e-book.

- Research online to see if anyone has posted complaints or criticism about the service. An effective conversion service will have many satisfied customers posting on blogs and support forums.

- Look for a conversion service that offers good customer support and personal attention.

As an add-on to a self-published print book

If you are self-publishing your book as a printed book as well as an e-book, your publishing company probably offers e-book conversion services. For an additional fee or for a cut of the royalty on each book, most print-on-demand (POD) publishing services will convert your manuscript to an e-book format and make it available for sale. Compare services and royalties carefully before you commit yourself. The cut the POD service takes from each sale is probably higher than the percentage charged by an independent e-book service, and your POD provider might make your e-book available only on its own sales network, not other e-book stores. A POD service provider is likely to use an automated conversion process that meets minimal standards and produces a sloppy e-book, and it might charge an additional fee for making changes to your e-book.

If the POD provider owns the rights to your book, it also will claim the rights to your e-book for a certain period, which means you cannot publish it elsewhere.

E-Books in the Headlines

Apple conspired with major publishers to undermine its competition and raise e-book prices

In March 2012, the U.S. Department of Justice announced plans to sue Apple and major publishers Simon & Schuster Inc, Hachette Book Group, Penguin Group (USA), Macmillan, and HarperCollins Publishers Inc for conspiring to raise and control the prices of e-books. The announcement followed an investigation of a deal struck by Apple and the five publishers in 2010, just before apple launced the iPad and iBooks. In July 2013, a federal judge ruled that Apple violated federal antitrust law. The five publishers previously settled. Apple filed an appeal in 2014.

Selling your e-book on your own website

You also have the option of converting your manuscript to various e-book formats yourself and selling it on your own website or through emails or paid ads. This method might succeed if you have an established readership, but it is not advisable because you will not be able to list your books on e-book retailer sites. Readers will not find your books unless they find your website first. One exception might be J. K. Rowling, who plans to sell e-books of the Harry Potter novels exclusively on her own website, Pottermore (**www.pottermore.com**).

E-Books in the Headlines

Pottermore Heralds a New Era in Electronic Publishing

On June 23, 2011, J.K. Rowling made headlines by announcing an online venture called Pottermore. For years, Rowling had withheld the publication of her seven Harry Potter novels as e-books and downloadable audiobooks. Her new site bypasses Amazon and Apple by selling the electronic versions of her books directly to consumers in multiple languages. Bloomsbury, Rowling's U.K. publishers, and Scholastic, her U.S. publisher will receive some revenue from licensing, but the e-books books are being published under the Pottermore Publishing imprint. Pottermore CEO Rod Henwood says, "We want to make sure anyone who buys it can read it on any device," which means Pottermore must reach an agreement with Amazon, whose Kindle controls about 60 percent of the e-reader market.

The venture employs every available strategy to engage Rowling's fans. Rowling launched Pottermore (**www.pottermore.com**) with an announcement on YouTube, and the site officially opened for everyone in April 2012. Within the first three days after the Harry Potter e-books became available, sales topped $1.59 million. Visitors to the Pottermore site can read 18,000 words of additional Harry Potter content that was not included in Rowling's novels.

An online gaming experience developed by the company Adam & Eve takes visitors through animated environments where they can earn points and win real-world prizes such as magic wands sequestered throughout Britain and the United States. Visitors also can interact on the site and upload their own artwork.

Choosing a Title for Your E-Book

A well-chosen title helps sell your book, especially when potential readers are searching for books online. Your title should be catchy, interesting, and, at the same time, contain keywords that relate to the content of your book. The title suggests what the reader can expect from the book. A short title like "Guide to Fly Fishing" for a nonfiction book can be followed by a longer, more explicit title, such as "How to tie flies, select the best equipment, and read mountain streams." The title of a fiction book can be creative, but it should suggest something about the genre. If you are writing a series of books, the title should have a common thread a reader can recognize instantly. Examples are the Chicken Soup series of inspirational books and Sue Grafton's alphabet mystery series: *G is for Gumshoe, V is for Vengeance,* and so on.

Titles cannot be copyrighted, but you do not want to confuse your readers by giving your book the same title as another book. Some series titles are trademarked. Once you have some ideas for your title, search for it on Amazon.com, in search engines, and on WorldCat (**www.worldcat.org**) to see what other books or publications have similar names.

A title that starts with the letter "A" or "B" will appear near the top of alphabetical lists. Numbers also appear at the top of alphabetical lists, but they are harder to remember.

As a final test, ask friends and fellow writers what they think of your title. They might not react as well as you expected or might have better suggestions.

Cover Design

The covers of books are displayed online as small pictures. An e-book cover image needs to be interesting and clearly visible as a thumbnail image. Along with your book title, your e-book cover might be your one opportunity to capture a reader's attention and convince him or her to pay for your book. Many readers will skip over listings that do not have cover images.

Your cover is an important marketing tool — people do "judge a book by its cover." People tend to form an opinion on the book based on the title, the presentation, layout, and professionalism of the cover design. A cover that looks too amateurish, inappropriate, or poorly put together indicates the book will be amateurish, too. Some e-book authors pay artists hundreds of dollars for a professionally designed book cover because they believe it is crucial for successful sales. Ask a friend or family member who is well versed in graphics and image editing to help you design your cover, or look for a freelancer or art student on Craigslist (**www.craigslist.org**) or one of the freelance websites such as Elance.com, Sologig.com, Guru.com, or Hireanillustrator.com.

Browse through book listings on e-book retailer websites and observe which cover designs catch your eye. The best designs are simple enough to be understood on a small scale, and colored so they stand out. Light-colored covers will fade into the white or pale backgrounds of Web pages. Except for the title and your name, avoid putting text on the book cover because it cannot be read easily on a thumbnail image. Use shapes and colors that evoke the nature of your book.

You can find templates for designing your own e-book covers on sites such as EBook Template Source (**www.ebooktemplatesource.com/free-ebook-covers.html**), Cover Factory (**www.coverfactory.com**), and My eCover Maker (**www.myecovermaker.com**) (subscription-based templates).

If you are inexperienced at graphic editing programs, try a simple one, such as Corel™ PaintShop Pro®, which you can find in a free trial version from **www.corel.com** or Paint.net® (**www.getpaint.net**). You can create a surprisingly elegant cover with few elements, using something as simple as the careful placement of text, or text overlaying a photograph you snapped and uploaded. You can also use the tools in the free Picasa software program (**http://picasa.google.com**) to create a cover.

E-book cover do's and don'ts:

- Make use of white space. "Positive" and "negative" spaces move the eye around and add interest, as do highlights and shadows.

- Match your colors well. You do not have to refer to a color wheel, but be aware of whether colors clash or complement one another.

- Look at glossy magazine ads, especially those in artist, architectural, and high-fashion magazines. Pay particular attention to covers of books that have debuted in recent years.

- Be creative and unique.

- "Bad" is a subjective qualitative value judgment that varies depending on who is looking (or judging), but avoid "bad" photographs — those that are blurry, faded, or have little contrast. Those same criteria can be used purposefully and artistically to create a "good" image. Use your judgment as to whether a photograph is of poor quality.

ISBN Numbers

An International Standard Book Number (ISBN) is an inventory and identification code issued to each individual edition of a book for shipping purposes. Because e-books are not being shipped physically, you are not required to have an ISBN number for an e-book, but you might want one for several reasons. You cannot list your e-book on Apple's iBookstore or certain other e-book retail outlets without one. You also will need ISBN numbers to list your e-books in catalogs and directories, such as those used by libraries. ISBNs are not necessary for books you do not plan to sell on the open market, such as family memoirs, or for books you intend to sell entirely on your own website.

You cannot reuse the ISBN number from a printed version of your book; you will need a unique number for your e-book. Publishers such as Smashwords will assign you a free ISBN number. ISBN numbers are registered to the purchaser, so your e-book will appear with Smashwords as the publisher. You retain all rights to your book, and you are still free to submit your book to other e-publishers. Amazon and Barnes & Noble assign their own internal identification numbers to books published for Kindle or NOOK, so ISBN numbers are not necessary if you only are publishing through them.

Different editions of the same book receive different ISBNs

A single ISBN can be used on all versions of that book that are printed. For example, a single ISBN-10 and a single ISBN-13 are associated with the mass market paperback version of Stephen King's *Carrie* published in 2005 by Pocket; a different ISBN-10 and ISBN-13 are assigned to the hardcover version of *Carrie* published by Doubleday. If Pocket were to release an updated version of their mass market paperback version — for example, if Stephen King approved a different set of edits on that version — it would carry a different ISBN-10 and ISBN-13 than the prior version. If you are publishing your book as an e-book and a print book, you will need a unique ISBN number for each.

If you want to start your own publishing imprint (brand), or if you expect to publish a number of e-books, you can purchase your own ISBN or buy a block of ISBNs for future books. Purchase ISBN numbers through Bowker U.S. ISBN Agency (**www.isbn.org**), individually or in blocks of 10, 100 and 1,000. The ISBN website recommends that publishers purchase enough ISBNs to last them for five years. The more numbers you purchase, the less they cost, and you will be able to maintain the same publisher prefix for a longer period. If you require only a single ISBN, they are offered by Bowker Identifier Services (**http://myidentifiers.com**) for $125.

In 2007, ISBN numbers moved from 10 to 13 digits to accommodate their growing numbers. According to the ISBN website, the "X" that appears at the end of the number represents the number 10; the last number is referred to as a "check digit." The ISBN-13 has five parts: the prefix, group or country identifier, publisher identifier, title or edition identifier, and the check digit. The publisher must update information associated with the ISBN whenever a book goes out of print.

Do It Yourself or Hire a Professional?

Part of the appeal of e-book publishing is that it does not cost much if you do the work yourself. You do not have to pay thousands of dollars to a vanity press or a printing company to edit, typeset, and print your book. Major book retailers like Amazon and Barnes & Noble, and independent e-book publishers like Smashwords, have created a business model that transfers many of the functions of a publishing house staff to individual authors. As an author, you are responsible for the quality and appearance of your e-book and for publicity and marketing. The book retailer does its part by providing basic publishing software, a sales platform, and exposure to millions of potential readers. The readers themselves act as editors and publicists by deciding what kind of books they want to read and what topics are interesting. They generate a "buzz" by telling their friends and fellow readers.

When your e-book sells, you and the book retailers benefit. If your book is poorly written and amateurish, it reflects on you. No one is watching over your e-book to make sure it meets high standards or stepping in to edit or rewrite it when you fall short.

Just because you have the capability to do everything yourself does not mean you should. It might be worth investing in a professional cover design, professional editing, or a professional formatting service if the result is an excellent book instead of a mediocre one. You know your own strengths and weaknesses. If you are comfortable working in Microsoft Word or HTML, nothing will stop you from preparing your own text manuscript for conversion to e-book formats. If you know how to use a basic graphics program and image editing software, you easily can create your own book cover image. You easily can learn how to insert images into an e-book. If Facebook is your second home and you have your own blog, you already know how to launch a publicity campaign using social media. Detailed instructions are available on e-book publishers' websites and countless authors' blogs, user forums and writer community sites, as well as in how-to books.

You can find every kind of e-book publishing service on the Internet, from editing and formatting to complete e-book conversion and marketing. Many freelancers offer their services for reasonable prices.

Before you start work on your own e-book, spend some time browsing through e-book retail stores and looking at e-books on an e-reading device or on your computer. Look at other books in your genre to see how they are organized, what the text looks like, what kind of cover designs are used, and how they are marketed. Look at high-ranking indie books in various retail outlets. Those authors are doing something right, and you can learn from them. When you form a clear idea of what your book should look like, you will know whether you have the skills to produce it yourself or if you need professional help.

Even if you pay someone else to do the job, experiment with formatting and uploading your own manuscript. The more you understand about the process, the better you will be able to communicate with the person working for you. Many e-book publishers allow you to upload and preview an e-book without actually publishing it.

Established e-book authors caution against expecting too much when you first launch your e-book. You will not become a best-selling author just by making your book available online, even if it is an excellent book. Until you develop a good publicity and marketing strategy, you will not earn more than a few dollars per week from e-book sales. Keep this in mind when deciding whether to spend several hundred dollars for a conversion service.

Although professional editing, proofreading, and formatting can add substantial value to your e-book, be cautious about spending money for marketing services. Press releases and paid ad campaigns are effective only when they are targeted directly at potential readers. Some so-called marketing services sold by e-book publishing companies send your press release out to a general list of media outlets with automated email software. You will benefit far more by personally contacting your local newspapers and TV stations. Build your own media contact list, network with other authors, and develop personal relationships that can help you promote your e-book. Many e-book retailers offer a variety of free features to help to publicize your e-book, such as rating lists and reviews. Paid advertising on a book retail site will have more impact than ads on random websites and search engines. The services of a professional book publicist are expensive, but consider hiring a freelancer to help with some aspects of your marketing campaign, such as writing press releases. One worthwhile investment is paying an experienced Web designer to create your author website and Facebook page and set up social media.

CASE STUDY: SOCIAL MEDIA IS A VITAL MARKETING TOOL

Adam Taylor
Founder and CEO
MyWebsiteSpot
www.mywebsitespot.com
info@mywebsitespot.com

Adam Taylor is founder and CEO of MyWebsiteSpot, a company that helps professionals and small businesses create an effective Internet presence and grow their client bases through social media. Services include search engine optimization (SEO), Web design, Facebook design, e-commerce solutions, and marketing.

E-book sales rely on word-of-mouth advertising, so you need to make yourself and your book known to as many people as you can. Effective use of social media has a ripple effect — the news keeps spreading in wider and wider circles, and you reach more and more readers.

First, you have to make it easy for people to find you on the Internet. Buy your own name as a domain name if you can, and search for domain names that incorporate each of your book titles. Get a professional to design a good author website, and optimize it for search engines by incorporating important keywords and phrases in the text, as well as your book titles, names of your characters, and definitive quotes.

When you start to build link traffic to your website, direct all the links to the same page. When you are promoting a new e-book, it is OK to direct traffic to an inner page of your website dedicated to that title, such as www.yourwebsite/yourbooktitle. Use that same URL wherever you post a link to your site — your blog, email signature, reviews, articles, Facebook, or Twitter.

Facebook offers powerful tools to network and let people know about your book. You can create a custom-designed tab to showcase your e-book with embedded videos, book previews, and links to your author website and book pages. We use an application by Flipping-Book that lets people flip through ten or 15 pages of your book right on your Facebook page. Readers can buy your e-book with PayPal™, click through to retailer sites where they can buy your books, or buy through affiliate links. Anyone who "likes" you on Facebook becomes your fan and has immediate access to everything on your tab.

We also use Google search to locate the latest news articles about a particular topic and feed those links directly to your Facebook account wall twice a day, so your fans can find the most recent information on the subject.

Facebook ties together information from many sources, such as your author website, Twitter posts, and blogs. Facebook users can find everything in one place and share it with their friends with one click.

Many authors create their websites in Wordpress, which accommodates many design features and plug-ins.

We have an automation service for Twitter that can be targeted to specific geographical locations. It constantly monitors Twitter, and whenever someone tweets a particular keyword, your Twitter accounts follows them. For example, if your e-book is about parenting autistic children, and someone tweets the words "autism" or "Asperger," they will immediately receive a tweet like, "Parents report astonishing results with new home therapies for autism. Learn more at yourbookpage.com" Twitter allows an account to follow as many as 200 people per day. If the person does not follow you back within three days, your account automatically "unfollows" them. This is important because Twitter enforces a follower ratio — you cannot follow more people than you have followers.

Some authors let readers "pay" for an e-book with a tweet or a Facebook "like." As soon as the person sends the tweet or clicks the "like" icon, he or she receives a link for a free download. They can pass on the free offer to their friends or followers instantly. You might be offering the book free anyway, but this strategy will gain fans on Facebook or followers on Twitter.

Pay-per-click or paid ads may increase traffic to your site temporarily, but the traffic will die down when the ad disappears. Organic SEO is more effective at building permanent traffic to your site. Paid ads might be appropriate when you are launching a new book or promoting a special offer for a short, limited time. Remember that ad click-throughs do not necessarily translate into book sales — if you make your ad too interesting, many people will click on it out of curiosity but never buy. Try to place paid ads on sites where people are shopping for books, such as e-book retailers or book blogs. Monitor paid ads carefully for results, and do not overspend your marketing budget.

The single most effective thing you can do to promote a new e-book is to ask people to review it on their websites. Spend two or three hours on Google looking for blogs, networks, and communities that relate to the topic of your book, and make a list of contact names and email addresses. Send each one a personal email asking if they would be interested in reviewing your book. Sometimes a review just falls in your lap; sometimes a site may charge $25 or $30 to review your book. That is money well spent. Never send out a mass email — you can write a basic email query, but send it individually to each person.

Chapter 5

Working with Graphics in E-books

Plain text e-books are easiest to publish, but you can illustrate your e-book with graphics and photos if you are willing to take some extra trouble with formatting. The main characteristic of text in an e-book is that it is reflowable — it automatically rearranges itself to fit the screens of various e-reading devices. You cannot control the position of photos on a page as you would with a layout for a traditional print book. Instead, each graphic has to be anchored to the text where it belongs and centered so it is fully visible in the e-reader screen.

Smaller images work best in e-books because some e-reading devices, such as iPhones, have small screens. An image that takes up a whole page from top-to-bottom or side-to-side will not display properly in some e-readers and might cause glitches that confuse the reader. If you are publishing for a specific e-reading device, such as NOOK or Kindle, follow the instructions for formatting and inserting images to get the best results. If you are publishing with Smashwords or another distributor that provides your e-book in multiple formats, it is safest to stick to small, regular-sized images.

Color coded

Images display on digital screens in RGB (red, green, blue) color, while printing uses CYAN color. Even though you have digital files of them, images especially prepared for a printed book might be in CYAN color, which will not display correctly in an e-reader. You will need to ask a graphic artist to rework and re-save your images as RGB.

Inserting Images in Your E-book

Before inserting images in your e-book source file, edit each one using an image-editing program to get the best possible image. Crop and balance photos, straighten horizons, sharpen images, and alter the contrast. See the section below on image sizes. Export digital photos for e-books from your camera software with a resolution of about 1024 x 768 pixels. Images from scanned photos or scanned printed images may appear grainy, blurry, or pixelated because the original is of poor quality or because a small image has been stretched or enlarged.

Almost any image-editing program can do the job — the software that came with your digital camera, scanner, or computer or a design program like Adobe® Photoshop® (if you own it). These free image editing programs produce good results:

Paint.NET (**http://paint.net**)
Originally intended as a free replacement for the Microsoft Paint program delivered with Microsoft Windows, Paint.NET began as a college student design project under the guidance of Microsoft. It includes photo-editing tools comparable to those found in commercial image editing software.

Google Picasa (**http://picasa.google.com**)

This software allows Google users to share their photos with friends and contains a variety of editing tools and special effects.

PhotoPlus SE (**www.freeserifsoftware.com**)
Offers many features similar to those found in Adobe Photoshop.

Save each image as a JPEG in a folder titled "[Title of your e-book] Images." After you have saved your images, click on each image in your folder and manually add the file extension .jpg to the image name.

If you are using Microsoft Word to format your source document, go to the place where you want to insert an image and click "Insert/Picture." Browse to the folder where your images are stored and click on the image you want to insert. Anchor the image by right-clicking on it with your mouse. Select "Format Picture," then click "Layout," then click "In Line With Text." Save, and then center the image using the Center button. In Word 2007, right-click on the image, select "Text Wrapping," then "In Line With Text," save, and center.

To make the image appear on a new page, click on the image. In Word 2003, use Format/Paragraph to center the photo as a paragraph. In later versions of Word, use the Paragraph settings on the Home. To keep multiple images consistent, create a special style for your image settings. When you have completed the formatting for an image, select the image and click on "Format," then "Styles and Formatting" in Word 2003. Click on "New Style" in the right-hand menu, give your style a name like "photo," and click "OK." In later versions of Word, click the bottom down arrow in the Styles box on the Home page, select "Save Selection as New Quick Style," and give it a name. Each time you import another image, click on it, and select the special photo style.

Size

An e-book resembles a website more than a print book. For a print book, high-resolution (high res) images are preferable because they show fine detail and nuances of color. In e-book publishing, and Web design, a high-res image has a large file size, is undesirable because it takes a long time to load in a screen, and requires more storage space. E-reader screens and computer monitors have low resolutions, so they cannot benefit from high-res images.

The terms DPI (dots per inch) and pixels sometimes are used interchangeably to describe the size of an image. DPI refers to the number of dots of ink a printer will print in a square inch (or centimeter) and has little to do with online publishing. Because a high-res image has a high DPI, when your e-book publisher advises you to use images of a specific DPI, it is ensuring the file size is not too large.

Computer monitors and e-reading devices display images in pixels, the smallest units of color that can be controlled on a display screen. Visualize a grid of tiny squares laid on top of your image. Each square in the grid represents a pixel. When you see a dimensional measurement such as 500 x 300 pixels, it is referring to a rectangle 500 pixels long and 300 pixels high. The pixels displayed by the screens of different e-reading devices might be different sizes, and some devices display larger numbers of pixels. As long as your images are within certain pixel dimensions, they will display properly on most screens. PPI (pixels per inch) refers to the density of pixels within a given area. A high PPI accommodates finer detail and more subtle nuances of color. The minimum PPI for display on e-reading devices and websites is 72 PPI. Smashwords recommends 96 PPI. Use one of these two numbers.

The amount of storage space occupied by a computer file is measured in bytes. A byte is approximately the space occupied by a single typed character. A kilobyte (KB) equals 1,024 bytes; a megabyte (MB) equals about 1 million bytes. Adding images to your e-book increases its file size, which means it will take longer for a reader to download and occupies more storage space in an e-reading device's memory. Text e-books without illustrations average about 1.1 MB. An average EPUB book file ranges from 3 to 5 MB. E-readers can download and store e-books of these sizes without problems. Much larger files, though, could take so long to download that they discourage readers from purchasing them.

The maximum source file size for conversion with Amazon KDP (Kindle) is 50 MB. NOOK Press accepts files up to 20 MB, Smashwords does not accept manuscripts larger than 5 MB. Check the size of your source document after you have inserted your images. You can do this in Microsoft Word by navigating to your file as though you were going to open it and right-clicking with your mouse on the file name. Select "Properties" from the bottom of the resulting menu. If your file is too large, you will be able to reduce its size by resizing your images or deleting some of them.

Use almost any image editing software to reduce the size of your images by following these steps:

- Convert other image file formats, such as BMP or PNG, to JPEG format. Open the image in your editor, then Save As with a .jpg extension.

- Compress your JPEGs. When saving your JPEG, most image-editing software will give you the option of compressing your image. You can reduce the file size as much as 75 percent by setting the compression level between 50 and 60 percent, without sacrificing the quality of your image. If your image editing software uses a compression scale from 1 to 12, set it between 6 and 8.

- Resize your image. In your image editing software, use the "resize" option to set a lower number of pixels vertically and horizontally before saving it as a JPEG. Do not try to resize by lowering the DPI of your image — doing this does not lower the file size.

If you are formatting in Microsoft Word, you can use the "Compress Pictures" option to compress all the images in your document at once:

- Click on any image to select it.

- Under "Picture Tools" at the top of the window, select the "Format" tab.

- In the "Adjust" section of the "Format" toolbar, click on "Compress Pictures."

- To compress all the images in your document, uncheck the box labeled "Apply only to this picture."

- Make sure that the "Use document resolution" radio button is ticked, then click "OK" to recompress your images.

Quick Tips on Creating Graphics for Columns and Tables in Adobe Photoshop or Fireworks:

- Open the document containing the text you want to create a graphic for.

- Select and copy the text by highlighting it and hitting Control + C (to copy).

- Open Photoshop or Fireworks®.

- Create a new canvas by hitting Control + N (or go to File > New).

- Choose the width and height. Try not to make it more than 450 pixels wide. You can adjust the length as needed by going to Image > Canvas Size. The resolution is fine at 72 PPI (pixels per inch). White is usually the default background; remember that Kindle screens show only grayscale (black and white), so it is best to keep the white background.

- With the text tool selected, draw a text box and hit Control + V to paste the copied text in the box. This is your first column.

- After sizing the first text column to your liking and adjusting the font size for readability (remember that the text should be large enough to be readable on a Kindle screen), remove the text to place in the second column by highlighting it and hitting Control + X to cut.

- With the text tool still selected, draw your second text column (in Photoshop you may have to deselect the text box first, or click another tool to deselect and then click the text tool again) and paste the text by hitting Control + V.

- Adjust the font size, column lengths, and text within each column until each column is roughly the same size. Make sure the columns have equal space around them vertically and horizontally, that there is a sufficient gutter (the space between the two columns), and that they do not appear uneven.

> • Save the document as a PNG (Fireworks default file extension) or PSD (Photoshop default), and then export as a GIF (best for images with few and less complex colors). Keeping the PNG or PSD file will ensure you have an editable file on hand in case you need to make changes.

Book Cover Images

Your book cover image will be uploaded to e-reading devices, online catalogs, and your website, book, and author pages, but you also might be asked to provide a high-resolution print image for magazine or newspaper articles. A good-quality print image of your book cover and your head shot should be part of your media kit. If you are hiring an artist to design your cover or exporting it from a design software program, request it as 300 DPI. You always can reduce the size and resolution of the image for your e-book, and you will have a good-quality print image to use on business cards, fliers, handouts, event posters, and anywhere else you might need it.

The cover image requirements of each e-book retailer are slightly different, but in general, the cover should have the same approximate dimensions as a book. It should be flat, not with a three-dimensional edge. The image should be crisp and clear and should carry the title of the book and the author's name. The cover should not have a price or URL on it. It should not include images of nudity, obscenity, or violence.

The artwork on your cover should be simple enough to be recognizable when it is shrunk to thumbnail size. Because thumbnails are square, some space on either side of your rectangular book cover will be blank. You might want to create a square version of your cover image to make maximum use of space in a thumbnail. A square image also can be inserted as a widget (a small icon that links to a website) on Web pages, social media, and in email to link readers to your book pages. A thumbnail is typically

125 x 125 pixels. You can obtain a thumbnail image by making a screenshot of your book cover

These are the cover image size requirements of several major e-book retailers:

Kindle:

- Minimum of 1000 pixels on the longest side
- Ideal height/width ratio of 1.6

NOOK Press

- JPEG file with a file size between 5 KB and 2 MB
- Sides must be between 750 pixels and 2000 pixels in length

Smashwords

- Recommend dimensions for inclusion in multiple retail sites: 925 pixels tall by 600 pixels wide
- Minimum height of 600 pixels

For many e-reading devices, your cover image should be inserted on the first page of your e-book, so readers see it when they open your book. EPUB and MOBI formats automatically insert a cover image before the first page of a book, which causes your cover to display twice at the beginning of your book if you have inserted it in your source document.

If you are formatting your e-book for a specific e-reading device or application, consider creating a cover that matches the exact proportions and dimensions of that e-reader, so it fills the entire screen.

PROPORTIONS AND DIMENSIONS OF E-READER SCREENS			
Device	Screen height in pixels	Screen width in pixels	Height/width ratio
iPad 1	1024	768	4:03
iPad 2	1024	768	4:03
iPhone 3GS	480	320	3:02
iPhone 4 / iPod Touch	960	640	3:02
iRiver Story	800	600	4:03
Kindle 4	800	600	4:03
Kindle Fire	1024	600	9:11
Kobo™ eReader Touch	800	600	4:03
Motorola Xoom	1280	800	16:10
NOOK Color	1024	600	5.12:3
NOOK Simple Touch	800	600	4:03
Samsung Galaxy Tab 10.1	1280	800	16:10

Glyphs

You can separate chapters or sections by inserting a small graphic image called a glyph. A glyph can be a black and white symbol or a simple illustration relating to your topic.

Ӝ♥Ӝ

Insert the glyph just as you would a photo or graphic, and create a specialized style setting (see above) to center it. Do not overuse glyphs because they can become distracting in a small e-reader, and keep the file size of the image small.

Chapter 6

An Introduction to E-Book Formats

ike all emerging technologies, several groups of programmers and developers created e-reading software using different approaches to solve the problems of displaying printed text and graphics on a screen. The result is that different brands of e-reading devices support different file formats.

The owner of an e-reader has to buy books sold through the manufacturer's bookstore or books in the format(s) supported by that particular device. For example, other devices cannot read e-books in Amazon Kindle's proprietary format, AZW, unless they are converted first to another format. Kindle or NOOK software applications (apps) can be downloaded and installed on some devices, allowing them to function as Kindle or NOOK e-readers.

You must convert your e-book manuscript to the format used by the e-bookstore that will sell your book. This is not difficult. You first create your manuscript as an HTML file or a Microsoft Word document and upload it to the website of the e-publisher/retailer, which will convert it to the format(s) used by that publisher. Some free e-publishing sites like Smashwords (**www.smashwords.com**) convert your manuscript to multiple formats and distribute them to many e-book retailers. E-publishing conversion services charge fees to prepare and format your book professionally for sale through a range of e-bookstores. If you are doing your own formatting, you can start with one e-retailer, such as Amazon.com, and add your book to other e-publishing sites as you gain experience or upload your book to an e-book distributor.

On the chart below, you can see which e-reading devices use which formats. As the market for e-reading devices develops, a movement toward a universally accepted format will build. You can expect each manufacturer eventually to make its e-reading devices universally compatible. No manufacturer of e-readers wants to lose sales because potential customers prefer books available through a competing e-bookstore.

Formats Used by Popular E-reading Devices

Name	Manufacturer	Bookstore	No of titles	Formats
Kindle	Amazon	Amazon	1.6 million	Kindle (AZW, TPZ), EPUB, PDF, TXT, MOBI, PRC DOC and HTML through conversion
NOOK	Barnes & Noble	Barnes & Noble	2.5 million (including Google books)	EPUB, PDB, PDF, TXT, DOC, PPT
iPad	Apple	iBooks	200,000	EPUB, PDF, HTML, DOC (plus iPad Apps, which can include Kindle and Barnes & Noble readers)
BeBook	Endless Ideas BV	All bookstores	All titles	Open source, compatible with all major formats. Widely used outside the U.S. global market
Kobo Wireless E-reader	Kobo	Kobo Store, but compatible with many formats		EPUB, PDF and MOBI book formats; PDF document formats; TXT, HTML and RTF text formats; JPEG, GIF, PNG, BMP and TIFF image formats; and CBX and CBR comic book formats

Name	Manufacturer	Bookstore	No of titles	Formats
Pandigital Novel	Pandigital	Barnes & Noble	2.5 million (including Google books)	PDF, EPUB, and HTML
iPhones	Apple	Any		Several iPad apps available for e-readers including Kindle and NOOK

Major E-Book Formats Explained

Every e-publication format consists of several components:

- A manager for the contents of the document

- Files that organize the material for presentation and give instructions to the e-reading device

- Navigation files, such as menus that help the reader move around in the e-book

- Files that allow the reader to set bookmarks, make notes, and link to other content

When you convert a book to a particular format for e-publication, all of these files are created and zipped together automatically into a single package. The major file formats used by e-reading devices are described below. Each was developed from a different origin, and each has advantages and disadvantages.

EPUB

EPUB (electronic publication) is the publishing format used by most major e-book retailers, including the Apple iBookstore, Amazon, and Barnes & Noble. An EPUB file is a zipped file comprising XHTML documents, packaging files (instructions for how the individual files are to be organized and displayed, and information about the author and publisher), and container files for encryption and digital rights management.

The text in an EPUB file is reflowable, which means it automatically arranges itself to fit the page size of any e-reading device, and resizable, which means the reader can increase or decrease the font size for easier reading. EPUB files can accommodate inline raster images (composed of pixels) and vector images (composed of lines). They contain embedded metadata (information about files and documents). EPUB incorporates CSS (Cascading Style Sheets), separate files that define fonts, headers, and other formatting used throughout a document or Web page. EPUB also supports DRM.

EPUB is maintained by the International Digital Publishing Forum (IDPF) (**http://idpf.org**), a global trade and standards organization. Its members include academic, trade, and professional publishers; hardware and software companies; digital content retailers; libraries; educational institutions; accessibility advocates; and related organizations that are committed to making digital content easily available to everyone.

The predecessor of EPUB, Open eBook Publication Structure (OeBPS), was developed by members of the IDPF (originally OeBF) and released to the public as an open, royalty-free standard in 1999. Since then, two versions of the specification have been published, the latest in 2002. OeBPS rapidly has increased the amount of e-book content available to consumers by making it possible for publishers and e-reader manufacturers to format e-books for publication without having to go through a long period of research and development.

E-book retailers like Barnes & Noble and Apple iBookstore will convert your book automatically to EPUB format when you upload it to their publishing websites. Each store takes a cut of the sales price for each book you sell through its website and pays you the rest as your royalty. The process of uploading a manuscript to be published as an e-book is simple, but you can encounter complications getting the book to appear exactly as you want it to in an e-reader, especially if your book includes illustrations, tables, or images. Each e-book publisher/retailer website gives step-by step instructions for preparing and uploading your manuscript, offers technical guidance and user forums to help solve problems, and recommends professional formatting services that will do the work for a fee.

Instead of uploading your manuscript individually to several different e-retailer sites, you can upload it to a publisher/distributor such as Smashwords, which converts your book to EPUB and several other formats for free and distributes it for sale through Barnes & Noble, Apple, Kobo, and other e-book retailers as well as on its own site.

If you want to sell an EPUB book directly from your own website, or if your book contains graphics and complex formatting and you want to experiment with arranging it before you publish, use a free EPUB conversion service such as 2epub.com (**www.2epub.com**) or Word2EPUB (**www.web-books.com/Publishing/Word2EPUB.htm**).

Do-it-yourselfers with some basic knowledge of software programming can find instructions for creating an EPUB file manually on the IDPF website (**http://idpf.org/epub**).

When you have finished creating your EPUB document, you can test it for errors using Google's Epubcheck (**http://code.google.com/p/epubcheck**).

E-Books in the Headlines

EPUB3 and KF8

Just in time for the 2011 Christmas season, both Amazon and Barnes & Noble released enhanced e-readers, the Kindle Fire and NOOK Color, that have many of the same features as tablet computers, including wireless Internet access, color displays, and the ability to play audio files, movies, and videos. The newest version of EPUB (EPUB3), released in October 2011, incorporates the latest Web standards, including HTML5 (additional HTML markup code that allows imbedded audio and video files, and inclusion of tables and charts) and CSS3 (the code that defines the appearance of Web pages in an Internet browser). EPUB3 allows full use of the features in NOOK Color, such as insertion of animations and video files. Many in the e-book publishing world were hoping that EPUB3 would become a universal standard, and that Amazon would embrace it for Kindle devices. Instead, Amazon released Kindle Format 8 (KF8) the same month, also integrating HTML5 markup code and CSS3. KF8 replaced MOBI and allows e-book authors and publishers to add many features and enhancements to their e-books.

MOBI

MobiPocket Reader software was developed from PalmOS, a format originally created for use in personal digital assistants (PDAs). Amazon purchased Mobipocket, the company that produces the software, in 2005. Mobipocket files have either ".mobi" or ".prc" extensions because PalmOS supports only PRC files. The two file types are so similar that you can convert one to the other by typing in the new extension name.

You can read Mobipocket books on the Amazon Kindle as well as in Amazon Kindle apps on Mac OS X, the iPhone, Android devices, Windows, and Windows phone devices. You also can read them using third-party software programs such as Lexcycle Stanza, Calibre, or Okular. Amazon offers a free program, KindleGen, which can convert or create documents in the Mobipocket format, thus Kindle owners can convert books and documents from other bookstores.

MobiPocket software allows the reader to make notes, comments, and bookmarks. Text cannot be printed or exported from MobiPocket; it must be manually copied and pasted to another document.

AZW

AZW (thought to stand for "Amazon Word") is a slightly modified, highly compressed version of MobiPocket used exclusively on Kindle and Kindle apps. AZW files have the extension ".azw". AZW has proprietary digital rights management (DRM) that allows Amazon to display a book only on devices registered to the account that bought the book. Unprotected AZW files can be converted to Mobipocket by simply replacing ".azw" with ".mobi." You can submit personal files to Amazon to be converted to AZW so they can be read on a Kindle.

AZW format includes auxiliary files with the extension ".mbp" that store things like bookmarks, annotations, last read position, and extra metadata. (Metadata refers to notes and technical information about the book, such as the date of publication, software used to create it, source files, keywords, and dates when it was modified.)

TPZ

Topaz (TPZ) is a format unique to Amazon. It is more flexible and has fewer restrictions than AZW, allowing larger images and font sets and characters that are not standard to Kindle. Topaz files have the extension ".tpz" or ".azw1" (for TPZ files delivered via Whispernet) and the auxiliary files that store notes and bookmarks have the extension ".mbp" or ".tan."

A Topaz e-book page is a collection of glyphs (visual images of small sections of text) along with annotations recording their position on the page and additional information that allows the page to be searched. TPZ automatically converts scanned text images of print books to e-books, which means many older books, along with the illustrations and charts they contain, can be prepared quickly for publication.

PDF

PDF (Portable Document Format) files are photographic images of pages. A PDF file preserves the look and layout of the pages of a printed book. Each PDF file contains a complete description of the document, including layout, graphics, fonts, and page numbers.

PDF was developed by Adobe Systems in 1993 and released as an open standard in 2008. For many years, e-books have been made available as PDF files that can be opened or downloaded and read with a computer. PDF is used widely to share business documents and scientific papers.

PDF documents can be read on e-readers, but they are not reflowable — the text does not adjust to fit the e-reader. You navigate through PDF documents by scrolling through them and moving from page to page. You can change the text size by zooming in and out. PDF documents do not display on e-readers as nicely as other formats, but PDF is useful in cases where it is important to preserve the graphic layout, for example, illustrated children's books, comic books, or scientific articles with numerous citations and page references. PDF also can be used for books you intend to sell only from your website because you do not need the services of a third-party vendor.

You can create PDF files using Adobe design software or convert a scanned or a text document to a PDF file. Documents created in Word 2007 or 2010 can be saved as PDF files. You also can find software applications on the Internet that will convert text documents to PDF files. When you self-publish a print book, you typically convert your finished manuscript to a PDF file before uploading it to the publishing company website.

Text formats

Text documents, such as Word documents, can be read on any computer, Web browser, or e-reading device. The earliest e-books were text documents that could be opened and read on a computer using word processing software. They were sold as computer discs, and later, when the Internet developed, as email attachments or downloadable files.

Text files have a fixed number of characters (usually 80) in each line, which makes them difficult to read on smaller e-reading devices. To get around this, they can be converted to a variety of other e-book formats using on-line converters available on numerous Internet sites. Once converted to a new format, the text becomes reflowable and wraps automatically from one line to the next.

Rich text format (RTF) preserves formatting, such as bold and italics and indentation. Plain text files do not.

Project Gutenberg, a volunteer effort begun in 1971 to archive cultural works as digital files, offers more than 38,000 free books as of November 2011, most as text files. The text format is crucial to Project Gutenberg's goal of making e-books accessible to as many people as possible. Preserving books in text format also ensures they will continue to be accessible far into the future, when the formats supported by e-readers and other devices will have gone through multiple transformations.

HTML

HTML (hypertext markup language) is the format used for most Web pages. In addition to the text content, an HTML file contains markup language — annotations dictating how the page is structured and how the text is presented to the viewer. For example, <bold>fish</bold> will display on the Web page as **fish**. The markup language is hidden from the viewer.

You can write the annotations in HTML files manually using plain text in the same way you type the text content of the document. Many software applications, including word processors, automatically insert the markup language when you select formatting options from menus as you type. Images and other objects can be embedded in an HTML file.

E-books written in HTML can be read in a Web browser. Many e-book publishers ask you to upload your manuscript to their websites as an HTML file, which they convert to the format(s) they use.

Calibre: Convert any format for your e-reader

A number of free software (freeware) programs will convert Kindle e-books and documents in other formats to EPUB so you can read them and organize your e-book library on any type of e-reading device or application. The best known of these is Calibre (**www.calibre.com**), created by Kovid Goyal. Calibre is a comprehensive tool for management of digital texts. It is used in more than 200 countries and volunteers have translated it into a dozen languages. It is a vibrant community of booklovers, committed to keeping e-books accessible and preventing the e-book market from becoming fragmented by commercial booksellers.

You also can use Calibre to open and preview your e-book on your computer before you publish it.

E-Books and Print Books

Formatting a manuscript for publication as an e-book is different from formatting for print publication. For print publication, a layout artist determines exactly how each page is going to look, with chapter titles and page headings, page numbers, a table of contents, charts, references, footnotes, illustrations, sidebars, and maybe even a special decorative font for the first letter of each chapter (drop caps). If you have formatted your own manuscript for publication through a POD service, you understand the pains you must take to start each chapter on a new page, and to make sure your references to other parts of your book contain the right page numbers.

You have no control over the appearance of individual pages in an e-book. The text in an e-book is reflowable, which means it adapts itself to fit the screen size of individual e-readers, as well as the personal font style and size preference of each reader. A few pages on a tablet-sized e-reader might turn into 50 pages of large print on a cell phone. Page numbers are no longer applicable; your table of contents and any references to other parts of the book hyperlink to the relevant sections of the text. In e-book publishing, your goal is to make your book attractive and easy to read on a wide variety of e-reading devices. To accomplish this, you will need to remove much of the formatting found in a print manuscript, such as styles, headers, footers, and forced page breaks. You still can use footnotes, illustrations, and special effects, but they must be achieved in a different way.

Preparing your e-book as a Microsoft Word document

Most e-book conversion/retailer services give you the option of uploading your e-book as a PDF file or a Microsoft Word document, which is then converted to HTML. Unless you intend to sell your e-book only as a PDF, it is better to upload a Microsoft Word document because it will convert more consistently to HTML. Before uploading or converting your Word document, clean the formatting up as much as possible so the e-book will look exactly like the document you create. (You do not have to do this if you are using a paid conversion service, as all the formatting will be done for you.)

If you previously formatted your book for POD self-publishing, you inserted section breaks, blank pages, page headers, and page numbers. Now you have to remove all those things to publish your manuscript as an e-book. Read your e-book conversion/retailer's formatting guidelines carefully before you begin.

To clean up a document previously formatted for print publication in Microsoft Word:

- Delete blank pages, headers, and footers. Take out any page breaks you inserted to keep paragraphs together and any hard returns that you used to position quotes or inserts.

- Your book should now begin with the title page. On the copyright page, type in the new ISBN number and insert the following information: [Service provider] Edition, published [date] by [Your name or the name of your publishing company].

- Make sure you use the same style throughout the document. You accidentally may have created new styles while trying to format.

- Change your margins to 1" or less and line spacing to 1.5 so the manuscript takes up less space in the reader screen.

- Make your manuscript HTML compatible by setting the font size at 10 point or 11 point and choose Arial, Tahoma, or Verdana as the font. Remove any strange characters or symbols. HTML is much simpler than modern word processing programs. It accommodates indented text blocks, bulleted or numbered lists, simple tables, and bold and italics, but not much more.

- Create a hyperlinked table of contents using the Word Table of Contents feature. Select "Use Hyperlinks Instead of Page Numbers" and set the drop-down levels to "1."

Apps

Books from the Kindle bookstore in AZW or TPZ format only can be read on Kindle e-readers. To read a Kindle or a NOOK book on a computer, iPad, or other brand of e-reading device, you can use software applications (apps) that duplicate the functionality of a Kindle or NOOK. Apps can be downloaded and installed on Android-based e-readers and can convert cell phones and tablet computers into e-reading devices. Once the app is installed, the reader can use many of the features available on the actual e-reader, such as annotations and links to online communities, if the device being used has the right capabilities.

Free apps are available from the various e-bookstore websites, and third-party apps can be purchased for specific electronic devices such as smart-phones and iPhones.

Some magazines and periodicals are published as apps, with interactive features and content that can be updated automatically. Traditional publishers like Penguin are developing books published as apps, which will be interactive and function something like computer games or online communities. E-books also can be published as iPhone apps, which allow readers to access the content much as they would a website. For example, a field guide for birds could be made searchable by species, description, color, and habitat, with audio recordings of each birdsong.

The concept of a book published as a software application opens the door to features that never could be made available in a print book. For example, a textbook can become an online tutorial, with reviews and quizzes, interactive vocabulary games, printable flashcards, and personalized tracking of the student's progress through the material. A how-to book can contain video clips demonstrating how to perform tasks and procedures. A children's book can read the story aloud as children follow along and include music and songs.

Digital Rights Management (DRM)

Now that you know all the different programs and file types associated with e-books, how can you ensure your e-book is protected from those trying to read it without properly compensating you? Do you even want to protect it in such as way? For the answers to these questions, we look to digital rights management (DRM) software. This software allows e-book distributors to control who gets to see a book and when. DRM-protected books only can be opened and read after a customer has paid for them. DRM can prevent a book from being printed or copied and tie it to a particular e-reading device so that it cannot be read on any other device. It also can limit the number of times a customer can download a copy of a book onto e-reading devices.

Free e-books do not require DRM because anyone can download them at any time. Tens of thousands of books are offered free by e-bookstores and websites, either because they are in the public domain (no longer under copyright protection) or because the author or publisher has chosen to make them free. A new release by a popular author, however, must be protected by DRM — otherwise no one would pay the $10 to $25 price to read the new e-book.

DRM is carried out using a variety of techniques. Encryption makes text files illegible unless they are opened using special software activated by a signal from the e-book distributor. Tags may be inserted within e-book files instructing the e-reading device how to respond to commands from its owner. Digital watermarking hides personal information about the buyer among the files of the e-book. E-reading devices or programs retrieve these bits of information and respond to the hidden instructions. Some DRM technology, including that used by Microsoft eReader, discourages e-book buyers from distributing their e-books to others by linking the buyer's credit card information to each e-book. If illegal use of the e-book is discovered, the original purchaser can be charged again for another copy.

An e-book file protected with one kind of DRM software cannot be opened and read on an e-reading device equipped to work with a different kind of DRM. There are three major types of DRM software in the market today: Adobe Content Server, FairPlay, and Kindle's proprietary DRM.

- **Adobe Content Server**

  Adobe Content Server protects EPUB and PDF files and uses encryption to prevent a file from being read until the book has been paid for. Many publishers and distributors of e-books in EPUB format use it. Publishers can select options that allow certain amounts of text from a book to be printed or copied or prevent printing and copying altogether. Adobe Content Server also allows e-book owners and libraries to "lend" books to other e-reading devices for specified periods. While a book is out on loan, the original owner is not able to access it. Patrons of many public and university library systems now can check out e-books and read them on their e-reading devices or computers. When a library purchases an e-book, it is buying the rights to a specific number of downloads. E-books borrowed from a library typically expire at the end of three weeks if not renewed.

- **FairPlay**

  Most of the books sold on Apple's iBooks store are encrypted with FairPlay DRM, originally developed to limit the number of times a song bought from iTunes® could be copied.

- **Amazon Kindle**

  Amazon's DRM is an adaptation of the original encryption used by Mobipocket for PDAs and business documents. Customers who buy a book from the Kindle bookstore can copy it onto as many as six devices registered with the bookstore. If the author or publisher has enabled its lending feature, a Kindle book can be loaned once to another reader for 14 days.

DRM has other uses besides regulating how e-books are opened and read. It is used to protect confidential or sensitive files and documents from being opened and read by unauthorized persons, to administer online classes and exams, and to control employee access to business documents within a company.

Traditional publishing houses use DRM to manage sales and downloads and protect their investment in their authors' e-books. Most e-book publishers and distributors give self-publishers the option of choosing whether they want their e-books protected by DRM. A small fee is added to the wholesale cost of each e-book to cover the extra expense. Adobe Content Server charges publishers more than $6,000 per year for a license, plus $0.22 for each e-book sold. You must make the decision to apply DRM before the e-book is published; otherwise, unrestricted copies of your book already will be circulating in the market. If you decide to add DRM after an e-book has already been published, you will have to withdraw the book and republish it.

A debate over the wisdom of using DRM is raging continually among self-publishers of e-books. Some believe the protection of copyright and intellectual property is important, and that DRM is essential for preserving the value of books and the livelihood of writers. Other authors believe that the publicity they gain from having their books passed around freely by admirers has far more value than the few sales that might have been lost because someone obtained a copy of a book without paying for it. Some of the arguments against using DRM are:

- The slightly higher price necessary to cover DRM protection, along with the difficulties of transferring DRM-protected e-book files from one type of e-reader to another, discourages buyers.

- The average price of an e-book is so low that most readers are willing to pay it even though they could get an unprotected copy from a friend.

- Hackers have found ways around all DRM protections anyway.

- If someone really wants to steal your book, they can retype the text or make screen shots of the pages.

- Most customer service problems with e-bookstores and problems using e-readers involve DRM.

- If you discover that someone else is selling copies of your book, or that your book has been plagiarized, you have legal recourse under copyright law, whether your book is DRM-protected or not.

DRM Could Have Long-Term Consequences

Consumer rights organizations have further concerns about DRM. When you buy a DRM-protected e-book, your ownership rights are restricted. You are not free to resell the book after you finish reading it or to pass it on to a friend to read on his or her e-reading device. DRM-protected books are difficult to transfer from one brand of e-reader to another. If you decide to replace your Kindle, you might not be able to transfer the books you bought from the Kindle bookstore. E-book retailers actively administer DRM; as time passes and retailers go out of business or merge with other companies, the books you bought from them might become inaccessible. Some technologies will become obsolete. DRM also gives the e-book retailers control overpricing, stifling competition, and shutting out independent retailers.

The decision whether or not to protect your e-book with DRM depends on your business model. If you want your book to circulate freely and be accessible on every kind of e-reading device, do not use DRM. Many e-book novelists benefit more from building large communities of fans, who eagerly await their next release, than they would from strictly controlling who can read their books. On the other hand, if you have invested a great deal of time and money in research, written a book with proprietary information or reports or plan to sell subscriptions to regularly updated content, you will need DRM to manage access to your book. Textbooks, travel books, how-to books, and scientific papers are all candidates for DRM.

CASE STUDY: CHILDREN'S BOOK AUTHOR DISCUSSES EBOOK IMPROVEMENT

Nik Perring
nikperringwriter@gmail.com
http://nikperring.blogspot.com
www.nperring.com

Nik Perring is a writer and workshop leader from the UK. His short stories have been published widely in places including Smokelong Quarterly, 3 AM, Metazen, Ballista, Word Riot *and* Dogmatika. *He is the author of the children's book,* I Met a Roman Last Night, What Did You Do? *(Educational Printing Services Ltd., September 2006).*

To be honest, the process of getting my book published in the mainstream print market was pretty straightforward. I had an idea for a book for children — historical fiction, based on the National Curriculum (UK), which would be educational. After I'd finished it and felt it was good enough to be "Out There," I started looking for a publisher whom I thought would be interested and happened upon Educational Printing Services, Ltd. (that specialize in educational books). EPS was the only publisher I approached, and they liked what I did, thought they could sell it, and offered me a contract very quickly. There were edits to do and bits that needed rewriting, which all went smoothly. About a year after I'd initially approached them, my book *(I Met a Roman Last Night, What Did You Do?)* was published.

I like the idea of e-books. I think they're going to be a considerable part of publishing's future. But they're not quite there yet — I think they've got quite a distance to go before they begin to reach their potential and usefulness. For them to get closer to that potential, I think three things need addressing.

First, the electronic readers, the devices the e-books are read on, need to be a good deal cheaper. (I think it's fair to say that a significant majority of those who have bought electronic readers are both book and gadget enthusiasts — that's not a sustainable market, nor is it one that's going to grow too much, especially with the limited choices of content on offer.)

Second, the titles themselves need to be cheaper. There's much to be said for having the ability to carry around with you a whole library of books, but that becomes less appealing when the electronic versions of those books are almost as expensive as their physical equivalents. As I see it, electronic readers will be practical companions to physical books — the two will exist side by side and will not, on the whole, be competitors. That means that I, as a consumer, might want to own both the electronic and physical versions of certain titles (so I can take old favorites on holiday, for example, without the extra weight and bulk). If I've already bought one at, for argument's sake, $14 (recommended retail price) I wouldn't want to pay a similar price for the electronic version, simply for the convenience of having it on my electronic reader (which I'll have already forked out a couple of hundred dollars on). One way around this, and an idea I'm fond of, would be to offer people who had already purchased one version of a title the opportunity to buy the other at a reduced rate.

Third, availability and choice need to be improved. For this whole electronic thing to work I, as a consumer, with varied and eclectic tastes, need to have access to pretty much everything I have access to via bookshops (on and offline) if not more. I'm primarily a short-story writer and was disappointed to find that Lorrie Moore, one of the most important and popular short story writers of the past three decades, had only one book (a novel) available from the Kindle Store when I searched for it on my iPhone's Kindle app (January 2010). There also needs to be one form of e-book file — so I can buy it from whichever retailer I choose and be able to download it onto whichever electronic reader I happen to own. And that's without mentioning the potential for out-of-print books and individual short stories and poems. Quite simply, the more stuff that is available, the more potential there is for sales, and the more reasons people will have for wanting to join the "electronic book club."

I think publishers, manufacturers, and retailers need to look at the iTunes/MP3 model, as opposed to VHS and Betamax. If I have an iPod, I can transfer what I've already purchased to it without buying the whole album or song again. If I want to buy something new, I have a considerable choice of where I can buy that from — a choice that's not dictated, or limited, by the sort of MP3 player I own. I think that's the scenario the electronic book world should be pushing toward.

However, do I see any benefit to publishing an e-book version of my existing title? No, I don't (not that I'd complain if my publishers wanted to put out an electronic version — I'm just not convinced there's a market for that particular book in that particular market just yet). I think that electronic readers are, at the moment, something that adults, rather than children, will own (because of their price) so I don't see how I or my children's book would benefit.

What I do think, though, is that there's an enormous potential market for this in the future, especially with educational books. If the electronic readers are affordable and the books interactive, with links to encyclopedias, course notes, textbooks, and the like, they could be of huge benefit to those in education and even could change the way things are taught. We've already seen how well the iPhone's worked in classrooms, after all.

So, yes, I like the idea of e-books and I think there's much to look forward to in the future; they have enormous potential to add to the world of literature, and I'm looking forward to that potential being realized, or at least, being approached.

Chapter 7

Publishing for NOOK with NOOK Press

To format your e-book for the B&N NOOK, you will use Barnes & Noble's NOOK Press self-service Web portal at **https://www.nookpress.com**. Your e-book will be made available through BN.com, NOOK eBook Readers, and NOOK eReading software for iPad, iPhone/iPod touch, Mac, Android, PC, and other devices.

Currently, you must have a U.S. bank account, credit card, and a U.S. tax ID (Social Security number) all tied to a U.S. address to publish on NOOK Press. Your e-books will be offered for sale only to U.S. customers. You must own the U.S. rights to your book to sell it at BN.com. If you own the copyright to your book, you automatically own the U.S rights. However, if you have licensed your e-book to another publisher or have previously published it through a POD publishing service, you may not have the rights to sell it in the U.S. Verify this with your publisher.

You are free to publish the same e-book simultaneously through other e-publishing sites.

You can read the entire *eBook Publication and Distribution Agreement — NOOK Press* online at (**https://www.nookpress.com**).

Pricing and Payment

You can set a list price for your e-book between $0.99 and $199.99. You will receive 65 percent of the list price for any e-book priced at or between $2.99 and $9.99, and 40 percent for any book priced at or below $2.98 or at or greater than $10.00 (but not more than $199.99 and not less than $0.99).

Your list price cannot be higher than your list price on any other e-book sales channel or than the list price of any print edition.

BN.com sometimes may offer customers a discounted price for your e-book as part of a promotion. In these cases, you still will be paid 65 percent or 40 percent of your list price for that e-book.

Content Restrictions

Barnes & Noble reserves the right to determine whether your e-book (including your e-book file, cover image, and product data) complies with its content policy. It will remove an e-book from its store if it deems the content "illegal, libelous, infringing, offensive, harmful or potentially harmful, threatening, harassing, legally obscene, defamatory, or intentionally hateful in any regard."

It will not allow:

- **Pornography** (Hard-core material that depicts graphic or explicit sexual acts)

- **Libelous material** (Material that intentionally harms or has the potential to harm an individual or a third party)

- **Copyright infringement** (Material for which you do not own the copyright or the right to distribute)

- **Advertisements** (Material contained within an e-book that primarily seeks to sell a product other than the e-book itself)

The description of your e-book (product data) is also subject to content restrictions. You may not include:

- Hyperlinks of any kind, including email addresses

- Any "call to action" (for example, a phrase asking readers to review your book or "like" you on Facebook)

- Advertisements or promotional material (including promotions for author events, seminars, or commercial products)

- Contact information for the author or publisher

You may publish public domain content with NOOK Press, but Barnes & Noble can, at any time, request validation that a given e-book qualifies as a public domain title.

Preparing Your Manuscript

You can use the word-processing and editing software on your computer to prepare your e-book for publication on NOOK Press. NOOK Press is a self-contained Web portal that works with an Internet browser. It is optimized to work in Microsoft Internet Explorer® 7, 8, 9, and 10, Mozilla Firefox 3.6 and later versions, Google Chrome 8 and later versions, and Apple Safari® 5.

If your book contains complex formatting, such as tables, graphics, illustrations, and visual effects, NOOK Press recommends uploading it as an EPUB file after you have previewed it in Adobe Digital Editions or Barnes & Noble's NOOK for PC application (**www.barnesandnoble.com/u/nook-for-pc/379002322/?cds2Pid=35114**) and verified that it looks the way you intend it to. Consider paying a conversion service to format the book for you in EPUB, so you have a perfect file. You can access the *NOOK Press EPUB Formatting Guide* on the Internet at **http://cp-barnesandnoble.kb.net/kb/?ArticleId=4327&source=Article&c=12&cid=28 #tab:homeTab:crumb:7:artId:4262**.

NOOK Press also has a free tool that will convert Microsoft Word (DOC and DOCX), HTML, RTF, and TXT files into EPUB. You will be able to preview your titles on a NOOK simulator before submitting them. Formatting guides for each type of file are available on the NOOK Press website.

NOOK Press offers the following tips for successfully formatting a Word document for conversion through its EPUB tool:

- Use Times New Roman, Arial, or Courier New font.

- You can use bold, italic, underline, and strike-through.

- You are allowed to insert links to other parts of your book and links to outside websites in a NOOK e-book. However, readers will not be able to directly access external websites while reading on NOOK Touch.

- Include only a single return between paragraphs. Do not use "Enter" to add extra space between paragraphs; use the Word paragraph tool instead.

- Do not use the "Tab" key to indent paragraphs. Set up a first line indent using the "Word Paragraph" tool.

- Do not insert page breaks. Start a new page with the "Section Break" option from within the "Page Setup" option.

- Use Microsoft Word's "Bulleted List" tool to make a bulleted list.

- To create a numbered list or multilevel outline, use Microsoft Word's built-in "Numbered List" tool.

- If you want text to appear in all capital letters, use caps lock. Do not use the Word format for all caps.

- For small caps, type in all capital letters and change the font size for the text area that will appear in small caps. Do not use the Word format for small caps.

- Do not use columns.

- Do not use superscripts and subscripts.

- Use Word margin controls to indent block quotes or large segments of text.

- Images can be formatted flush left, flush right, or centered.

- Wrap text above and below an image, not around the image.

- Avoid using most symbols because they will probably appear as question marks.

- Type fractions as numbers instead of the automatic Word format for fractions.

- Create tables in portrait rather than landscape orientation to make them fit on the page.

Uploading Your Book to NOOK Press

When your manuscript is ready for publication, create an account on the NOOK Press website (**https://www.nookpress.com**). Log in using your Barnes & Noble account login. If you do not have a Barnes & Noble account, create one using the link under the sign-in box. When you have filled in your name, address, and financial information, you will be taken to the NOOK Press publishing site. On the "My Titles" tab, click "Add a Title." Fill in your author details, and browse to your manuscript file on your computer. Click "Upload," and "Preview." The file must be smaller than 20 MB in one of these formats: EPUB, HTML, RTF, TXT, DOC, or DOCX. When the file has finished loading, a pop-up window will appear with a preview of your NOOK book. Go through each page to see how your book looks.

You then will be prompted to upload your cover image. The cover image must be a JPEG file between 5 KB and 2 MB. The sides of the image must be between 750 pixels and 2,000 pixels long. *Follow the guidelines in Chapter 8 for book description, product information, and pricing.*

When your book is ready, click "Put on Sale." It will take 24 to 72 hours for your book to appear in the NOOK store.

Making formatting changes and editing your NOOK book

If you are not satisfied with the way your book appears in the NOOK preview, you can make changes and upload it again. Either go back and make changes to your source document, or download the EPUB file that NOOK Press has converted for you from the "Add a Title" page and edit the HTML. When you have finished your changes, click on "Browse" to locate the revised file and then click "Replace & Preview" to view it again on the NOOK simulator.

You can make changes to your NOOK book after it has been published by uploading a new file and clicking "Put on Sale." Again, it will be 24 to 72 hours before your book becomes available for sale. During this period, you cannot make additional changes.

Customers who already have purchased your NOOK book will retain the old version in their e-readers. They will receive the new version only if they delete and reload the book or if they load the book onto a new device.

Reviews, sales ranking, and other products are all linked to your book by its exact title. If you make changes to the title, you will lose this information.

If you encounter formatting difficulties or cannot figure out how to make a graphic or table appear the way you want it, you might be able to find assistance from other users in the forums on the NOOK Press. Help Board (**https://www.nookpress.com/support/faq**).

Marketing on Barnes & Noble

Once your book is available on the Barnes & Noble website, you can post a NOOK Press icon on your website, blog, or Facebook page that will take readers directly to your product page.

The BN.com customer review system allows readers to post feedback easily about your book. A star rating system shows potential buyers at a glance how popular your book has been with other readers. Encourage your readers to rate your book; the more stars a potential buyer sees next to your title, the more likely the possibility that he or she will choose to purchase your book. Positive reviews also help sell your book. Each NOOK Press author has an author page on BN.com. Barnes & Noble encourages authors to make the most of their bio pages by listing awards and accolades, previous publications, and career details.

Chapter 8

Self-Publishing Your E-book on Amazon Kindle

Anyone can publish an Amazon Kindle e-book free. Your e-book will be made available for purchase through Amazon.com. Each time someone purchases your e-book, you receive 70 percent of the sales price, and Amazon keeps 30 percent. You retain all ownership rights to your work, and you are free to publish your e-book simultaneously on other platforms.

EPUB format can be uploaded to Amazon Kindle so your Kindle e-book does not need to formatted separately. You can use the HTML version of your EPUB file and follow the Kindle formatting guidelines to prepare it for conversion as a Kindle e-book.

Books are published for Kindle through Amazon's Kindle Direct Publishing (KDP)(**http://kdp.amazon.com**). If you do not have an Amazon account, open a free account by clicking the "Sign Up" button on the right side of the page and creating a user name and password. Once you have opened your account, you will be able to access the KDP pages as well as the Kindle formatting guides and user forums.

Content

Amazon Kindle does not accept some types of books. These include:

- Pornography or offensive depictions of graphic sexual acts

- Any content that Amazon deems "offensive"

- Content that violates laws or copyright, trademark, privacy, publicity, or other rights

- Public domain and content that is exactly the same, or almost the same, as one or more other books

- Books that "provide a poor customer experience"

Amazon reserves the right to determine which content provides a poor customer experience. Examples of books that might be excluded include those that are poorly formatted so that they do not display well in Kindle e-readers, books that promote merchandise, and books with misleading cover art, titles, or descriptions.

Formatting

Kindle Format 8, Amazon's newest Kindle format, incorporates features and enhancements that can be enjoyed on Kindle Fire and later-model Kindle e-readers, including colored text and backgrounds, drop caps, numbered lists, text that wraps around images, fixed layouts, nested tables, callouts, sidebars, and Scalable Vector Graphics (SVG) (graphics that retain their clarity when they are enlarged or made smaller). Books published in Kindle Format 8 resemble websites. CSS3 (Cascading Style Sheets), Kindle Text Pop-Ups, and Kindle Panel Views make it possible for you to create attractive children's books, picture books, and comics in addition to the traditional text e-book.

Your manuscript must be in HTML format for upload to KDP. Amazon strongly recommends using Microsoft Word to format your document, then saving it as an HTML file. Prepare your document in a single file that contains the entire manuscript or document from start to finish, from the front cover to the back cover. Start by pasting your text onto a blank Word document, and save it a .DOC or a .DOCX file. Now you are ready to format your manuscript. The Simple Formatting Guide on the KDP website (**https://kdp.amazon.com/self-publishing/ help?topicId=A2RYO17TIRUIVI**) will take you through the process step-by-step.

Like other e-reading devices, the Kindle is designed to re-flow and resize text automatically. Amazon recommends using little formatting in text files and using as few hard returns or hard line breaks as possible. Kindle will automatically justify your text (straight margins on both left and right) and indent the first line of each paragraph, so you do not need to format your manuscript this way to submit it.

Kindle Format 8 accepts many of the automated formatting features available in Word, including indentations, bold characters, italics, tables, and an active table of contents. Do not use bullet points, special fonts, headers, or footers because these will not be transferred to your Kindle book.

If you need to indent paragraphs manually, do not use the "Tab" key because this will not convert to Kindle. Instead, click on "Page Layout," and specify the amount of indentation in the "Indent" option. You also can use the tab on the ruler at the top of the page to change the indentation.

Click on "View" and check the "Ruler" option to make the ruler appear across the top of a Word document.

Instead of including footnotes, convert footnotes to hyperlinks that take readers to another section of your book, such as an endnotes section. Your readers also will find it helpful if you embed hyperlinks in your text to websites with supplementary information, especially for nonfiction works. Because the Kindle includes basic Web functionality, hyperlinks allow users to navigate directly to the URLs you mention. In Word, highlight the name of the link in the text, click on "Insert," then "Hyperlink," and type or paste in the URL. If you incorporate hyperlinks in your book, warn your readers in the book's front matter that navigating to image-laden websites might slow their device's functionality. Include links to your website, online bibliography, or blog in the front matter and at other appropriate places in your book.

Insert a page break at the end of each chapter to separate it from the next chapter. In Word, use the "Insert" and "Page Break" commands. You also can use page breaks to separate other sections of the book such as the title page and bibliography.

Create front matter (a title page, copyright notice, and perhaps some blurbs) and back matter (your author bio, information about your other books, even sample chapters). Format the title page by centering the text and using a larger font.

When you have finished all your formatting, save your document as an HTML file using the simple "Save As" command. Open your Word document, click "File," go to "Save As," and choose "Web Page" (Word 2007), or "Save as HTML" (Word 2003). Any images or embedded files will remain fixed in their proper positions.

You also can prepare your manuscript as a single HTML file. For more information on HTML or for help embedding images within the HTML document, see Amazon's Direct Publishing forum (**http://forums.kindle-directpublishing.com/kdpforums/index.jspa**). See *Appendix D: HTML Basics* for more information.

You also can upload a PDF file of your book, but graphics, formatting, page numbers, and sidebars in the PDF design do not always convert well to Kindle. Kindle is a flexible format that lets users set their own type size for viewing text, and the PDF format can be too limited for users to do this. To create a PDF file in Microsoft Word, you can choose "Save As" and select "PDF" as the file format.

The preview you see in the KDP after uploading material is not an accurate representation of how the document will look on the Kindle. To test the format, layout, and final presentation, you will need to publish and view the document on a Kindle or on Kindle e-reading software on your computer. Then you can make adjust your manuscript and republish your book.

Graphics and Images

KDP accepts the following image formats:

- **JPEG (.jpg)**
  JPEG images do not support transparency. JPEGs are best for photographs and images with fine detail and a lot of color. They can handle up to 16 million colors and cannot be animated.

- **Graphics Interchange Format — GIF (.gif)**
  GIF images support transparency and are used for animations. They can handle up to 256 colors and are best for illustrated graphics, those with large blocks of color, and those with few colors.

- **Portable Network Graphics — PNG (.png)**
  PNG images support transparency but cannot be used for animation. PNG-8 supports up to 256 colors and is best for drawn

graphics and clip art with few colors or images with large color blocks. PNG-24 supports up to 16 million colors and is best for photographs or images with a lot of color and fine detail.

- **Bitmap — BMP (.bmp)**

Cover images only can be TIFF (.tif) or JPEG format.

Upload color images if you have them. Kindle E-Ink devices with black and white screens will display images in 16 shades of gray for contrast and clarity. On other Kindle devices and applications, such as the Kindle Fire and Kindle for iPhone or PC, images will appear in color.

The Kindle file format internally supports JPEG and GIF images of up to 127 KB, allowing rich nuances in images or content with gradient patterns.

An HTML image with an aspect ratio of 9 to 11 automatically displays with maximum screen coverage. Images should not be too small. Please make sure your input photos are at least 600 x 800 pixels. Images of less than 300 x 400 pixels can be rejected. The first number, 600 in this case, always refers to the width, and the second number to length.

When you upload a DOC document with embedded images, KDP extracts images from the content and replaces them with HTML <img> tags. The images become separate files that are part of the e-book publication package.

The maximum file size for conversion through Amazon KDP is 50 MB. Files larger than 50 MB may fail to convert completely. If your manuscript file exceeds 50 MB, you can reduce the file size by converting all your images to JPEGs and compressing them. *See Chapter 6 for more information on how to compress your images.*

Book covers

Your book should have a book cover. *See Chapter 4 for more information on creating a cover for your e-book.*

Amazon provides these guidelines for book cover images:

- You must have a minimum of 1,000 pixels on your longest side, probably the height.

- Amazon uses a height/width ratio of 1.6.

KDP for Mac Users

Some Mac users experience difficulty with document conversion because Mac text encoding is unfriendly to the KDP system.

If you are using Microsoft Word or Apple Pages software on your Mac, you can create a Word DOC format file that will convert well to Kindle format. Be sure to "insert" images into your document rather than copying and pasting.

If you want to add more advanced formatting, you can convert your Word file to HTML and add additional HTML tags. You can create an HTML-version of your book in Microsoft Word by clicking "Save As Web Page" under the "File" tab. In Apple Pages, choose "Export" and "Send to iWeb" to export your file to HTML format.

Once your file is saved as HTML, edit it if needed in an HTML editor such as Taco, which can be downloaded at **http://tacosw.com**. Then, when your images are embedded in your HTML document and it is all finished and ready to upload, zip the entire document in its single file with a program such as YemuZip. YemuZip is free and available for download at **www.yellowmug.com/yemuzip**. Your file is now ready for KDP upload. Keep in mind that if you are using a character set such as Chinese, this will not work.

Uploading a Book Using Amazon's Kindle Direct Publishing (KDP)

Now, with your book in finished format, you are ready to upload to KDP. Make sure all images are embedded, and the copyright information, title page, table of contents, chapters, index, acknowledgments, and anything else you want to include in your book are in a single document and saved as an HTML file.

"My Shelf"

You are ready to begin uploading your document. At this stage, do one final check over your document to ensure that everything is in place. Then navigate to the KDP homepage, and click on the "My Shelf" tab at the top.

Add new item

Click the "Add new item" button to begin the process of uploading your work.

Enter Product Details

After clicking "Add new item," multiple form fields appear under the heading "Enter Product Details." If at any time after beginning to enter information you have to leave the document, click the "Save entries" button at the bottom right hand corner of the "Enter Product Details" form and sign out. The next time you sign back in, the new title will appear as a draft (under "Status"). Click the plus sign next to "Enter Product Details" to expand the form and begin entering information. If you need to delete the title and start over, click the "Trash Can" icon to the far right, next to "Draft." The following sections will help you fill in the fields that appear in your uploading process.

Title

Enter the full title of your work, including any subtitles. For example, in "How to Publish an E-Book: Everything You Need to Know Explained Simply," the portion of the title after the colon is considered the subtitle and should be included in the title field. A long title is not necessarily a hindrance as long it is specific, informative, and contains elements that can cause it to appear in a search.

Edition number

If this is the first instance of your title, type "First Edition" or simply "1" in the "Edition Number" field. Designate any subsequent editions appropriately, for example, "Third edition." If you have revised the book and are updating the title, it is considered a new edition. When you republish a manuscript after making a few minor corrections, it is not considered a new edition. Be sure to include this information in the description as well; for example, you might want to include a sentence like "This is the third revised, updated edition." Also, include the edition information with the title's copyright information on the copyright page if your title is a book. For example, a recent edition of the *Associated Press Stylebook* includes this information at the bottom of the copyright page: "First edition, August 1977" and on a new line directly beneath that, "46th Edition, 2011."

Series title

If your title is one in a series, enter the title. For example, if you are uploading a publication that is a printing of the winners of a twice-yearly fiction competition, enter the title of the publication and the competition name, for example: "Best Literary Review Fiction Competition."

Description

Provide as complete a description as possible in this field. For ideas, refer to descriptions of large publishers' books and to the book synopses (descriptions) that appear on the back covers or dust jackets of books. The description should be professionally written and include the highlights and most important details of the book. Be careful not to overexaggerate. If you build up readers' hopes and your book does not deliver to those expectations, you run a strong risk of receiving negative reviews, which can hurt your sales. The description is limited to 850 characters (characters include text, punctuation, symbols, and spaces).

Book Description Do's and Don'ts

Bad Description: *This book will change your life. Several experienced authors write about different ways to be successful.*

> How will it change your life? What is the topic? Who are the authors? Are they co-authors? What do they write about? What is their experience? Successful in what — life, business, or money?

Good Description: *One of the most sought-after actors of the 20th century and beyond, Johnny Depp has fascinated media and fans alike since the 1980s. Known for his unconventional roles and dashing good looks, Depp has earned international acclaim through movies such as* Edward Scissorhands, Secret Window, What's Eating Gilbert Grape?, Donnie Brasco, Pirates of the Caribbean, *and many more. His charming appearance, quirky sense of humor, and infamous affairs all have kept him in the limelight. Author Johnny Mayhem's unauthorized biography presents an insider's look at the life of this famous actor, from childhood to the present day.*

> This description provides specific details about the subject of the book and the topics discussed. The copy is written in a professional, appealing way.

Publisher

Enter the publisher's name; if this title has not appeared in print or otherwise through a publisher, enter your name in this field. It will appear more professional to enter a publisher title or your first and last name, rather than something like "Sandra's Publishing." If you have a URL set up for your writing and publishing or another professional Web address related to the title, publisher, or author, you can enter it here.

If you want to choose an original name for your "publishing company," it is a good idea to do a fictitious name search to make sure the name you choose is not already in use. Technically, you do not have to worry about this too much unless you are planning to use the name to form a business entity, but it cannot hurt to check in advance. Research business names on your state business website. For example, Florida residents can visit the Florida Department of State Division of Corporations website at **http:// sunbiz.org** and click the "Look up a Business Name" link in the left navigation area. If you want to use a name like "Red Hat Publishing," look up the name on your state business website to ensure it is available. Then do a search on Google to see if it is being used anywhere else. If you are self-publishing, you might choose a title that sounds more professional or simply use your last name — for example, Westmark Publishing.

Language

Enter the language this document is published in. If it is a translation, enter the language it appears in here. The place to mention that it is a translation and other relevant details (about the original language and author, for instance) is in the book description.

Publication date

Enter the date of the original publication. If this Kindle edition is the first time your title will be published, enter today's date in this field. If the title has appeared in another format, enter the first date it was published.

ISBN Numbers

Type the ISBN number in this field only if you already have an ISBN number for your e-book. *See Chapter 4 for more information on obtaining ISBN numbers.* If you are uploading material that has an ISBN number for a hard-copy version, you are supposed to use a different ISBN for electronic versions of the same work. However, if you use the same ISBN for the hard copy and electronic versions, you effectively can link all versions of the same document, whether it is in Kindle, paperback, or hardback version. This method enhances sales and integrates all data concerning the book, such as bibliographic information and customer reviews. If you do not have an ISBN, leave this field blank. Anything lacking an ISBN is assigned its own ASIN. ASIN stands for Amazon Standard Identification Number, and Amazon assigns it to every product sold through its website. If a book has a 10-digit ISBN (an ISBN-10), the same number is used by default as the ASIN. Both an ASIN and an ISBN are assigned for tracking and inventory.

Publishing Rights

You will be asked whether you own the rights to publish your book or whether it is public domain. If your rights are limited or if you have published the title under contract with a publisher or other company that holds foreign rights, you already should have checked with them or checked your contract to find out if you are within your rights in publishing the title. Depending on your contract, publishing for the Kindle might be something only your publisher has the right to do.

Categories

Under "Categories," click the "Add/Edit" button. This brings up a box that allows you to select the primary topics associated with your e-book. You are allowed a maximum of five categories. Selecting multiple topics helps add detail to your title's data and helps it appear accurately in a search. Scroll through the entire list to check all appropriate categories. Clicking on the plus sign expands the category; click on the open circle of relevant categories to select them. A green arrow appears indicating the topic is selected. Once you have selected all appropriate categories, click the "Add Categories" button in the center of the box to send the categories to the "Selected Categories" area. The "Delete" button allows you to remove unwanted or mistakenly selected categories. Once you are satisfied with your selection, click the "Confirm" button to close the window and return to "Product Details."

Author

Under "Authors," click the "Add/Edit" button. A box appears titled "Add/ Edit Contributors." In the drop-down menu, you can select from the following categories: "Author," "Editor," "Illustrator," "Narrator," "Photographer," "Foreword," "Introduction," "Preface," and "Translator." Type the person's name in the blank field on the left, and select the most appropriate designation from the drop-down menu. A "Remove" button allows you to delete an entry. Click the "Add Another" button to create a new field; the maximum allowable number of entries is ten. Be sure to add all relevant parties to the list, including all authors, contributors, illustrators, photographers, editors, and anyone else whose category is listed here or who contributed content to the title (including someone who wrote a preface or afterword). It is important to provide attribution to as many contributors as possible. Any persons beyond the allowable ten should be specified somewhere in the book copy, along with their contribution. When you are finished, click the "Done" button.

Search keywords

Enter five to seven descriptive, relevant keywords. Keywords help users find your title in a search. Think of the words or phrases that best describe your content, and separate them with commas. For example, if you are writing a book on health care for children, some of the keywords (and key phrases) you might use would be *children's health, health care, pediatrics, caring for children*, and so on. Successful keywords are those found in the overlap between two imaginary circles — one circle containing the words and phrases that are most likely to send searchers to your title and the other containing the words and phrases most commonly used by Amazon searchers.

Try starting with a free Google keyword tool, located online at **https:// adwords.google.com/select/KeywordToolExternal**. Select the radio button for "Descriptive words and phrases," and then type in a description of your title's content to get a feel for how keywords are generated. Also, visit the Amazon help page for key phrases, located at **www.amazon.com/gp/ phrase/help/help.html**. An example of a key phrase page can be found at **www.amazon.com/phrase/Johnny-Depp**. In this case, the page shows results for all products containing phrases related to Johnny Depp. Another option for finding keywords is to look at the keywords and key phrases associated with Amazon titles similar to yours.

Product image

Click the "Upload Image" button to upload your title cover. A box appears that allows you to upload the image from your hard drive. A notice provides a link to "Amazon's Product Image Guidelines" and warns you that images must be in either JPEG (.JPG) or TIFF (.TIF/.TIFF) format, and that they should be at least 1,000 pixels on the longest side.

Click the "Browse" button to select the file from your computer to upload. Once you have selected the appropriate file, click the upload button. If you are not satisfied with the image you have uploaded or have uploaded the wrong file in error, click the "Upload Image" button again to select a different file.

DRM

This is where the Digital Rights Management (DRM), discussed in detail in Chapter 5, is enabled. The options are:

- Enable digital rights management
- Do not enable digital rights management

If you choose to enable digital rights management, your file will be converted after clicking "Save entries" to adjust your content appropriately. Once your document is successfully converted, you will be prompted to click the "Preview" button. The preview document will appear in a format resembling the Kindle. It is important that you page through all the screens to check all the content. If you notice any errors, note the link at the top of the preview area that reads, "Download the HTML." Click this to download the file, make adjustments as needed, and upload again. If you need to make changes, be sure to check the preview file again after uploading to ensure everything displays properly. Some common errors that appear are extra spacing between sentences and stray punctuation.

After making this change, you will need to confirm your rights to upload the content for distribution. Click "Save entries" to complete the process. If you already have published your content and are changing your file, even in the process of reconverting it to enable or disable DRM, you will have to republish your work by clicking "Publish." If you do not take this step, your title will be listed as a draft. After republishing, your content will not be buyable for 24 to 36 hours. Generally, the content will become available in one to two hours. The delay is caused by the time it takes Amazon to update its global catalog, add the content to the search index, and update any other information that you may have changed before republishing, such as the product detail page.

Upload and Preview Book

Click the "Browse" button to locate the file on your hard drive that will be uploaded. Choose the final document, and click the "Upload" button. The document will process and should only take a few moments to upload for users with fast Internet connections. Once the document is processed, a notice will appear in a blue box letting you know the conversion of your document has been successful.

Preview

Click the "Preview" button to preview your converted document. Take the time to look through your document carefully, and make note of any conversion problems or other errors. Of course, a best practice would be to do a side-by-side comparison of the preview version with your original version. Watch out especially for such things as extra spacing and stray punctuation marks.

The "Product Preview" screen approximates a Kindle; you must click the left and right arrows at the top to navigate through the document. One problem you might encounter is an error message warning you there is a problem previewing your document. In that case, click the left arrow to return to the previous page and then navigate forward again.

Common errors might appear with line breaks and spacing. You have the option, via a link at the top of the "Product Preview" window, to download the HTML document your file has been converted into. Do this only if you are comfortable working with HTML. *See Appendix D: HTML Basics.* Otherwise, make the necessary changes in your document from your computer, save it, and then upload again it by clicking "Browse" and navigating to the file (be sure it already has been saved and closed) and clicking the "Upload" button again.

If you have saved and closed the file on your computer and clicked "Browse," but the "Upload" button remains grayed out, you will have to trick the system into allowing you to upload the newly updated document by clicking "Browse" and selecting a file of a different type than the file you just uploaded. For example, if you originally uploaded a Word (.doc) document, found errors, and corrected them in the document as your previewed the first version, make sure your corrected final document on your computer is saved and closed, and then click Browse and navigate to a file with a different extension, even one that is obviously wrong, such as a .jpg or .xml file. Click "Upload," and the system will give you an error message or, depending on the type of file you uploaded, will go ahead and open up the "Product Preview" window. You then can close out the preview window. If an error message comes up, click "Browse" again, and navigate to the corrected, final document. Click "Upload" again, and preview the document carefully. You can repeat this process as often as necessary until you are satisfied with your final document.

Enter price

Many considerations go into setting the price. Enter a price you think is fair but that will attract buyers. Consider the work's value and the pricing of the competition. Check out at least five or six comparable titles — they should be similar in length, form, content, and subject matter — and see how your price measures up. Many bestselling titles whose hardcover versions retail for $26.95 (or more) in the bookstore sell for $9.99 in their Kindle incarnations.

On January 15, 2010, Amazon administration posted new pricing guidelines in the KDP forums. The list price for a title now cannot exceed a print edition's lowest suggested retail price (set by the publisher), if one exists. Also, any digital books that are between 3 and 10 MB must be priced at a minimum of $1.99, and file sizes of more than 10 MB must be priced at a minimum of $2.99.

Once you are satisfied with the price you have set, click "Save entries" to save this information and proceed to publishing your document.

Publish

After entering the price, the "Publish" button in the top right corner of the screen becomes available (it is no longer grayed-out and becomes clickable). Click "Publish," and wait for your document to upload. It can take 12 to 72 hours for your content to become live in the Kindle Store and possibly even longer for your bibliographic data, cover art, editorial, category, and sales ranking information to arrive on the product detail page for your title. Until your title is processed, you will see a message under the "My Shelf" tab in the KDP that reads: "Publishing [Your Title]. Your book is currently under review by the Kindle Operations team..." and so on. The message warns that title updates take longer to process.

Troubleshooting, Editing, and Removing Published Content

Incorrect file formats or files that have trouble processing, such as PDFs, cause the most problems. *If you are on a Mac and have trouble uploading your files, refer to the section earlier in this chapter titled "KDP for Mac Users."* If you are experiencing a problem or issue not covered in this chapter so far, visit the KDP support forums to see if someone else has run into your problem, which is likely. View the support forums at **http://forums. digitaltextplatform.com/dtpforums/index.jspa**. On the main forum page, you can choose "Browse the Knowledge Base" or "Discuss in the Forums." If no answers turn up, search through Google. Many other forums and blogs address common problems encountered when publishing through the KDP.

Revising published work

You can download published content, if necessary, by navigating to the KDP homepage and clicking the "My Shelf" tab. Click the plus sign next to the document you need to modify, and then click the plus sign that appears by "Upload and Preview Media." Click "Preview" and "Download." You will be prompted to save the file to your hard drive. The file downloads as a zip file and is in HTML. Save the file, and then navigate to it on your computer. Of course, if you already have access to the copy, you can skip the preceding steps. If you are not familiar with HTML, you will want to work from the native file anyway. *See Appendix D: Basic HTML.*

Navigate to your file, modify it as needed, and then upload it again. If you downloaded the HTML file from the KDP, copy the edited file back into the ZIP file you downloaded. Make sure any images and other HTML content is saved in a single folder, as there can be no content in sub-folders. Then, click the plus sign by "Upload and Preview Media," navigate to the ZIP file, and click "Upload." To update content that already has been published, you must then take the additional step of clicking the "Publish" button on the KDP dashboard. After your updates are processed (this may take longer than the usual maximum of 72 hours for new content), your updates will be live in the Kindle Store.

Removing published work

To remove, or "unpublish" content, navigate to the "My Shelf" tab in the KDP dashboard. Click the plus sign that appears next to "Enter Price" (Step Three), and uncheck the box by the bold-print words "Amazon Kindle Store." The item will be removed within 72 hours and will disappear from the Amazon store after one week (minimum). You can republish the item by checking the box by "Amazon Kindle Store" and clicking the "Publish" button. Republished items appear in the store within 12 to 72 hours.

```
CASE STUDY:
INDIE WRITER GOES THE
WAY OF THE E-PUBLISHER
```

April Hamilton
www.AprilLHamilton.com
http://AprilLHamilton.blogspot.com
indieauthor@gmail.com

April L. Hamilton is an author, blogger, Technorati™ blog critic, leading advocate and speaker for the indie author movement, and founder and editor-in-chief of Publetariat, the premier online news hub and community for indie authors and small imprints. She has spoken at the O'Reilly Tools of Change conference and the Writers Digest *Business of Getting Published conference, and she has judged self-published books for competitions run by* Writer's Digest™ *and the Next Generation Indie Book Awards. She has been quoted in* The Wall Street Journal, MSN Money *and* The Washington Times, *profiled by ABNA Books and The Writing Cast podcast, and her book,* The IndieAuthor Guide *(released in an updated and revised edition from Writer's Digest Books in November 2010) has received favorable mention on* CNET *and* The Huffington Post.

In January 2010, I read that Martin Amis and Ian McEwan elected to go indie with e-book publication of their back catalog titles, rather than have them re-released through a mainstream publisher, largely because they can earn a 70 to 75 percent royalty going the indie route. Standard e-book royalty percentages offered by traditional publishers only run about 25 percent or sometimes 50 percent for more established authors.

As to the "why," I'd say it's a combination of factors. First, trade publishing is in crisis. Between struggling brick-and-mortar booksellers, the industry's unsustainable return policies, the pressures brought about by the e-book revolution and the recent flood of inexpensive and free e-books, the Google Books settlement, and their already historically narrow margins, trade publishers are facing simultaneous, unprecedented challenges. As a result, they've become more risk-averse than ever and have reduced author advances and marketing budgets, all of which leads to a much less author-friendly environment — especially for debut authors.

The second major factor consists of recent improvements in e-book and print-on-demand technologies that have made it possible for self-publishers to duplicate the quality of mainstream-published books without having to pay large up-front fees to a vanity press or sign away their publication rights. E-book publication is even simpler, and authors who publish their own e-books enjoy royalties 25 to 50 percent higher than those whose e-books are published by mainstream publishers.

The third factor is Amazon, which lists self-published books right alongside mainstream-published books and offers indie authors all the same sales tools and marketing opportunities as mainstream authors. Amazon is now positioning itself as a publishing channel alternative to mainstream publishers, and I don't doubt the move will be entirely successful for the company. The final factor is the decline of the chain, brick-and-mortar bookstore. Chain, brick-and-mortar booksellers always have been reluctant to stock self-published books, but now that those booksellers' market share is shrinking day by day, it's no longer critical to get one's book stocked by them. All of these factors are merging to make indie authorship a very attractive alternative to mainstream publication.

The decision of whether to self-publish is one that ought to be made on a manuscript-by-manuscript basis. It all comes down to three questions. First, what is the author's goal for the book? It's not always just about sales; sometimes it's about building readership or supporting a related activity, such as a speaking tour. Second, can a traditional publisher help the author reach her goal more quickly and effectively than the author could do herself? And finally, is the traditional publisher *going* to do the things that will help the author reach her goal more quickly and effectively than the author could do herself? For most authors, debut authors in particular, the answers to the latter two questions are increasingly, "no."

However, a niche manuscript can be a great match for an independent, niche publisher. For example, *Writer's Digest* Books published a revised and updated edition of my originally self-published book, *The Indie Author Guide*, in fall 2010. In this case, I decided that because my goal is for the book to be made available to as many indie authors (and potential indie authors) as possible, WD Books would help me reach my goal more quickly and effectively than I could do on my own. *Writer's Digest* is an established and trusted brand among authors and aspiring authors, and WD Books' catalog is limited to books for and about writers. WD is a forward-thinking company that is open to exploring new technologies and promotion avenues, and WD has numerous established outlets through which it promotes its authors and their books including magazines, websites, conferences, classes, and book clubs.

So, in this specific instance, I elected to go mainstream. However, I doubt I'd do the same with one of my novels because I think they would be lost in the crowd if I sold them to a mainstream publisher — especially a publisher that's just one arm of an entertainment mega-conglomerate, such as Viacom. Smaller, independent publishers have small catalogs, and as a result, they have more riding on every title they release. They're just as invested as the author in a given book's success. Because my fiction isn't really "niche" or genre fiction, however, it's not likely to appeal to a small publisher with a specific target demographic.

I started out going down the mainstream path and didn't have much difficulty getting a strong agent. Like most aspiring authors, at that point I thought the hardest part of the process of getting published was behind me, but I was wrong. My novel *Adelaide Einstein* got a stack of glowing rejections from the big publishers' editors, all of whom offered some variation on, "Of course *I* love it, but the American book-buying public doesn't want comic fiction right now. Send me something darker." So, I wrote a dark comic mystery, *Snow Ball*. My agent didn't like it and declined to go out with it at all. Life went on, and I forgot all about my novelist aspirations until a few years ago, when I entered *Adelaide* in the Amazon Breakthrough Novel Award contest on a whim.

After accumulating 36 positive Amazon customer reviews for *Adelaide*, I concluded New York editors don't have any idea what the American book-buying public wants and made the decision to go indie. I published both novels independently, first in Amazon Kindle editions and then in trade paperbacks via CreateSpace, Amazon's POD service. The experience was definitely a learning process for me, and because I have extensive experience with technical writing, I decided to document all I'd learned in another book, *The Indie Author Guide*. I became an outspoken advocate for indie authorship, which led me to found Publetariat.com, an online news hub and community for indie authors and small imprints. The site was an immediate hit, so I documented my processes for the design and launch of the site in another book, *From Concept to Community.*

I don't see much of a future for myself as a novelist in commercial terms, though I have a couple of fiction works in progress and hope to finish them eventually. I've come to the conclusion that promoting indie authorship and helping my fellow writers accomplish their goals through indie authorship is what I'm meant to be doing, and I've certainly found it very fulfilling.

Chapter 9

Self-Publishing Through a Distributor: Smashwords and Google eBooks

Distributor/retailers convert your e-book to a variety of formats and distribute it for sale through multiple e-book retailers, including Barnes & Noble, the Apple iStore, and sometimes Kindle, in addition to selling and promoting it on their own sites. To pay for these services, they take an additional cut of the sales price. Distributors make your book widely available through as many outlets as possible for as many e-reading devices as they can. Unlike Barnes & Noble and Amazon, their business models do not include the sales and development of proprietary e-reading devices. Instead, they focus on producing e-books that display well in almost any e-reading device.

Publishing through a distributor is the fastest and easiest way to get your self-published e-book into the market. On their retail sites, distributors offer many of the same promotions and sales features as the major book re-tailers. They also support active communities of indie authors who interact and share tips and experience.

Some paid conversion services act as third parties and format your manu-script for upload to an e-book distributor. Because distributors give de-tailed do-it-yourself instructions for formatting and uploading an e-book, nothing is stopping you from doing this yourself free. If you do not think you can do a good job because you lack formatting experience, hire a free-lancer to help you. Upload your own manuscript for publication and retain control of all your publishing accounts and settings.

Smashwords

Smashwords (**www.smashwords.com**) launched in February 2008 by Mark Coker, who was frustrated by his own attempts to find a publisher for his novel. It quickly became the leading e-book publisher for inde-pendent authors. 300,000 e-books and represents more than 90,000 au-thors and hundreds of small publishers. The number of e-books published on Smashwords continues to increase, from 140 books in 2008 to over 250,000 in November 2013.

Smashwords classifies itself as a distributor of e-books. It gives you the means to publish your own e-book, and then distributes it for sale through multiple retail channels. Smashwords converts your book free to nine for-mats. In addition to selling your e-book on Smashwords.com, it distributes books to most of the major e-book retailers, including the Apple iBook-store, Barnes & Noble, Sony, Kobo, and the Diesel eBook Store. Smash-words also has a distribution agreement with Baker & Taylor that enables Smashwords e-books to be read via the Blio eReader application, which makes Smashwords e-books accessible across an even wider range of de-vices and operating systems. Smashwords' agreement with Baker & Taylor also brings Smashwords e-books to public libraries that subscribe to Baker & Taylor's Axis360 digital media platform.

In addition, Smashwords places e-books in the sales catalogs of leading mobile e-reading apps such as Stanza (on the iPhone and iPad), Aldiko and Word-Player (on Android devices), FBReader, and the Inkmesh ebook search engine. Smashwords takes a commission of 15 percent of your net proceeds from each sale (the sales price minus PayPal processing fees) on Smashwords.com and Stanza, 10 percent of each sale made through other book retailers, and 18.5 percent of each sale made through its affiliate program. For sales made through major book retailers such as Barnes & Noble, Smashwords takes only a 10 percent commission, so you receive 60 percent of the list price of your book. Payments are made and received through PayPal.

The advantage of publishing with Smashwords is that you prepare and upload your manuscript only once to make it available through multiple outlets, bypassing the complications of managing several individual accounts with different retailers. Publishing through Smashwords is a quick and easy way to get your e-book on the market, and the company provides free ISBNs. The disadvantage is that you do not make quite as much from each sale as you would by uploading your manuscript directly to individual booksellers' publishing sites.

Smashwords' Standard Catalog contains all the e-books sold on Smashwords.com, and its Premium Catalog distributes to major online book retailers. Inclusion in both is free. To be listed in the Premium Catalog, an e-book must meet higher formatting standards and have an attractive cover, a professional book description, and proper copyright information. Because a large portion of Smashwords e-books are sold through the online retailers, try to get your book into the Premium catalog.

A third catalog, Atom/OPDS Catalog, distributes all the books sold on Smashwords.com to the native catalogs of major mobile app platforms. A few thousand books that have sold more than $1,000 on Smashwords.com are distributed directly to Amazon Kindle.

You do not have to have a U.S. address and bank account to publish on Smashwords because payment is made through PayPal. However, non-U.S. residents automatically have 30 percent income tax withheld on each sale.

Income tax exemptions for non-US residents

The UK, Canada, and Germany have treaties with the U.S. exempting their residents from paying income tax on income made in the U.S. Other countries have partial exemptions. To claim this exemption, you must send Smashwords a signed U.S. IRS Form W8-BEN. You first will need a signed letter from Smashwords to get a U.S. tax identification number (ITIN) by submitting U.S. IRS Form W7. The whole process is complicated; wait until your book is selling well before starting it.

When you upload your manuscript to Smashwords for conversion, you can select which file formats to convert to. If you want to distribute your book through major retailers such as Barnes & Noble, you must select EPUB, which is the format they use to display books in their e-reader devices. The MOBI format is distributed to Amazon. Smashwords strongly recommends selecting MOBI because many Kindle owners buy their e-books directly from Smashwords instead of through Amazon. Some formats are not suitable for certain types of books. For example, images will not appear in TXT and PDB files, so if your book is essentially a picture book, do not publish in these formats. You will be able to go into your Smashwords profile and disable these formats after you publish, if you discover that your book is not displaying well in some of them.

Smashwords does not publish:

- Partial or incomplete books
- Book covers with pornographic titles, depictions of nudity (artistic or photographic), or depictions of graphic violence (These will be rejected automatically by major retailers.)

- Erotica involving children

- Public domain books

- Books with content that is published elsewhere under other authors' names (Books must be original works, and the author or publisher must own exclusive rights.)

- Books whose primary purpose is to sell another product

Smashwords uses a proprietary automated e-book conversion technology called "Meatgrinder" to convert your manuscript into multiple formats. Meatgrinder works well with books that are mostly words, such as fiction, narrative nonfiction, and poetry. Pictures and images can be inserted in your e-book, but they may not appear exactly as they did in your manuscript, or they may alter the formatting somewhat. You may have to make several attempts to get your book to appear the way you want it. Comics and picture books will not convert well. Meatgrinder also does not support tables or columns, so any charts of this type will have to be inserted as graphic images. *See Quick Tips on Creating Graphics for Columns and Tables in Adobe Photoshop or Fireworks in Chapter 8 to learn how to create a chart as a graphic image.*

Formatting for Smashwords

All you need to prepare your manuscript for conversion on Smashwords is a computer with a word processing program such as Word. Smashwords strongly recommends using Microsoft Word (the file will be saved with a .doc suffix). Any version of Word will do the job. It is possible to create an acceptable file using the free OpenOffice word processing program, but you probably will have to work out some glitches.

Smashwords founder Mark Coker has written an 89-page *Smashwords Style Guide*, available free on Smashwords.com, which takes you step by step through the process of formatting your manuscript for publication through Smashwords. Only books formatted according to the *Smashwords Style Guide* are eligible for distribution through its major e-book retail partners, so download a copy and follow it carefully. By formatting your manuscript according to the *Smashwords Style Guide*, you will be able to produce an attractive, good-quality e-book almost instantly. The purpose of the *Smashwords Style Guide* is to make sure your e-book looks good in as many formats as possible, so it can be read with a wide variety of e-reading devices.

Smashwords Style Guide contains illustrations and detailed instructions for using various features of Microsoft Word to format your e-book manuscript. Essentially, the process goes like this:

- Create a working copy of your document in Microsoft Word by saving it under a new name. Keep the original version of your document so you can refer to it or start over again if something goes wrong.

- Turn off the "Track Changes" feature in Microsoft Word.

- Turn on the "Show/Hide" feature so that all formatting code in the document becomes visible.

- Turn off Microsoft Word's "AutoCorrect" and "AutoFormat-As-You-Type" features to prevent the insertion of unwanted formatting as you work.

- Use "View/Print Layout" to find and remove all text boxes from your document.

- Follow instructions to set a consistent "Normal" paragraph style for your entire document. Microsoft Word's style features automatically create a variety of paragraph styles and headings based both on templates and on the way you manually format your document as you are typing. These styles can insert unwanted formatting and cause your e-book to look strange. Setting a "Normal" paragraph style will give you a consistent font, line justification, and paragraph style throughout your document. The "Normal" settings in your version of Microsoft Word may have been altered, so you must check the underlying settings of the "Normal" style to make sure you have the correct font size, type, and line spacing.

- Select one method for separating paragraphs in your e-book: **first-line indents** or the **block text** method. Fiction and many types of narrative nonfiction books indent the first line of each paragraph, without placing a blank space between paragraphs. Some nonfiction books display each paragraph as a block of text, separated by a blank space from the paragraphs above and below it. If you do not distinguish the paragraphs in your e-book, they will run together in the e-reader and create an unpleasant reading experience. Follow the instructions in the *Smashwords Style Guide* to set your "Normal" paragraph style for either first-line indents or to define a trailing space that will automatically insert itself after each paragraph. Once you have set your paragraph style, you can begin a new paragraph by hitting the "Enter" key on your computer keyboard to insert a paragraph break. The formatting symbol ¶ indicates a paragraph break in your document.

First line indents look like this:

She opened her eyes and became aware of a dazzling brightness filling the room. The morning sun was pouring in through the window above her bed.

Outside, the roar of the surf could be heard in the distance. Some children were playing just underneath her window, and hearing their shouts, she felt excited anticipation for the day ahead.

Block paragraphs look like this:

> *Before planning any kind of lesson, define your objectives. What do you hope to achieve with this lesson? What particular knowledge or skill do you want to impart? What knowledge will the student have acquired by the end of your lesson?*

> *Next, define the capabilities of your students. How much background knowledge do they have in this subject? Are they already familiar with technical terms and vocabulary? What is their reading level? How long can you expect them to concentrate?*

Do not use the "Enter" key to position text on a page, and never insert more than four consecutive paragraph returns because this creates blank pages in some e-reading applications.

- Add bold text, centering, and italics where needed. Customized styles can be created for specific purposes such as formatting chapter titles, centering images, or arranging lines of poetry. Using customized styles for repetitive formatting tasks will keep the appearance of your e-book consistent.

- Add hyperlinks to your document. Some e-reading devices allow readers to click on links to go to outside websites for additional information. You also can use hyperlinks to connect the reader with other sections of your book. Smashwords recommends careful use of hyperlinks because too many can distract your reader away from your book. They also create a navigation hazard on a touch screen — if your reader inadvertently swipes across a hyperlink, the e-reader suddenly will jump to another page.

Hyperlink to your own website or your personal Smashwords page. Do not insert hyperlinks to specific book retailer sites — this is inconsiderate of the other retailers who will be marketing your e-book. Hyperlinks to affiliate marketing pages are a violation of Smashwords' Terms of Service and will cause your account to be deleted immediately.

- Add navigation to your book. Smashwords accommodates three types of navigation: an NCX (Navigational Control for XML) file, a linked table of contents (TOC), and internal links to endnotes, footnotes, and other sections of your book. The NCX is part of an EPUB file and generates the navigational menu that appears on your e-reading device and helps you find your way around your book. NCX files are required by many e-reading applications. Smashwords automatically generates an NCX file during conversion, based on chapter titles or your linked table of contents. If it is unable to do this, it will create a simple, two-part NCX file pointing to the beginning and the middle of your book. The *Smashwords Style Guide* contains detailed instructions for creating a linked TOC. Test your navigation links in Microsoft Word before you publish and afterward in various e-reading applications.

- Add front matter and a title and copyright page. If you have "blurbs" — short quotations or excerpts from book reviews praising your book — you can insert them at the beginning of your manuscript. Limit the amount of space devoted to blurbs, your book title, introductory illustrations, and your table of contents because some e-book retailers offer only a small percentage of your book as a free sample for potential buyers. If the first 15 percent of your e-book is taken up by front matter, your readers will never get to sample enough of your book to become involved in it.

  Smashwords is strict about the format of your copyright notice. Your copyright page must include the words "Smashwords Edition" or "Published by (your name or the name of your publishing imprint) at Smashwords." Keep your title/copyright page simple. It should include the book title, author name, "Smashwords Edition," and the words "Copyright 201_Your Name." You also can insert a link to your Smashwords author page.

- Add back matter to your book. The end of your book is a good place to tell readers about yourself. Include a short biography and give them links to your Twitter account, Facebook page, and your Smashwords author page. If you have published multiple books on Smashwords, include hyperlinks to your other titles and even some sample chapters.

The size of your formatted manuscript file must be smaller than 5 MB. To check your file size in Microsoft Word, click "Open," and navigate to your file wherever it is located in your computer. Right-click on the file name, and select "Properties" at the bottom of the menu. The resulting screen will show you the file size. If your file is larger than 5 MB, it probably contains large images or too many images. Consider whether any unnecessary images can be removed and reduce the file sizes of essential images.

Five most common Smashwords formatting mistakes

According to the *Smashwords Style Guide*, the most common formatting problems that cause e-book manuscripts to be rejected are:

- Using tabs or the space bar to indent the first line of each paragraph

- Using the "Enter" key more than four times to move text down the page. This will create blank pages in a small e-reading device.

- Using both an indent and a blank line to separate paragraphs. Set up a paragraph style for your document.

- Using outsized, colored, or non-standard fonts

- Failure to include the required copyright information

To make your book as attractive and easy-to-read as possible, Smashwords strongly recommends:

- Aligning text to the left margin of the page. This alignment is sometimes referred to as "ragged right" by its detractors because it leaves an uneven right margin to accommodate words of different lengths. Microsoft Word's "justify" feature will spread out the words in each line to create an even margin on both sides; this often results in uneven blank spaces between words that are distracting to the reader's eye and might produce unwanted effects in a small e-reading device.

- Keeping font sizes simple and uniform. Limit the number of font sizes in your manuscript, and make your headings and chapter titles just one font size larger than the body text. Large font sizes may occupy too much space in a small e-reader, and jumping from large to small words is hard on the eyes.

Book cover

Your formatted manuscript is now ready to upload to Smashwords, but do not upload it until your cover image is ready. Your cover is an important component of your marketing strategy and is required for distribution through the Smashwords Premium catalog. Publishing your book without a cover image will make a bad first impression on potential readers and cause you to lose valuable opportunities to sell your book.

Your cover image should be an upright rectangle resembling a book, at least 600 pixels tall (the ideal dimensions are 800 pixels tall and 500 pixels wide). The book cover should include the title and author name in letters large enough to read when the image is shrunk to thumbnail size. It should not include a price or a Web address. Avoid nudity and obscenity. The image should not be grainy or pixelated.

Publishing on Smashwords

When your manuscript is ready for publication, you can upload it to Smashwords by clicking "Publish" on any of the Smashwords Web pages. Follow the instructions.

Once you publish your e-book to Smashwords, it goes through an automated review by the Smashwords AutoVetter and then a manual review by the Smashwords team. If your e-book is rejected during one of these reviews, you will have to make corrections to your manuscript and upload it again. Go through the *Smashwords Style Guide* carefully and verify that you followed all the steps. The rejection notice may contain suggested changes. After you have made changes to the formatting, upload the manuscript using "upload new version" link in your account Dashboard, and then click the button to resubmit it for consideration. Following Smashwords standards guarantees that your e-book will look professional and be easy to read in any e-reading device.

If you encounter difficulty formatting your e-book for Smashwords or find that it is taking too much of your time, you can hire an experienced formatter to do it for as little as $25 an hour. Obtain a list of Smashwords formatters and cover designers by emailing list@smashwords.com.

Smashwords policy on piracy

Smashwords contends that e-books sell most successfully when they are made easily available, in a variety of formats, to as many potential readers as possible, and when readers appreciate and support their authors. Smashwords does not administer DRM. Instead, it recommends educating readers by placing a Smashwords License Statement on the copyright or title page of the book, reminding them that they have an ethical and legal obligation to the author. For paid books, ask unauthorized readers to go to Smashwords.com and purchase their own copies of the book. A free book can contain a statement authorizing distribution for noncommercial purposes or inviting the reader to visit your author page on Smashwords.com and learn about your other books.

Because e-books are less expensive than print books, most readers are willing to pay for a book that they enjoy and benefit from. Overpricing your book, however, might encourage piracy.

Pricing

Smashwords allows you to set the price for your e-book on Smashwords. com. All of the pricing options on Smashwords may not be available if your book is going to be distributed to major retailers. The Smashwords "Reader Sets the Price" feature allows readers to decide how much they are willing to pay for your book. Barnes & Noble does not accept any "Reader Sets the Price" books. For other commercial retailers, the price of these books automatically defaults to $4.95. All prices on Apple must end in $.99 – your price automatically will be raised to the next $.99 when your book is distributed to the Apple store.

Marketing opportunities on Smashwords

Smashwords emphasizes its role as a leading publisher and retailer of in- die e-books and encourages its authors to participate actively in its online community by writing thoughtful reviews of other authors' books, joining writers' groups, and posting in its forums. Many Smashwords readers are loyal supporters of Smashwords authors. Founder Mark Coker has written a *Smashwords Book Marketing Guide*, available free on Smashwords.com (**www.smashwords.com/books/view/305**) offering 30 useful tips on how to maximize marketing opportunities for your e-book.

In addition to distributing your book to multiple retailers and mobile read- ing apps, Smashwords offers a number of promotional tools:

- A customized author page and a book page for each of your e-books, optimized for search engines, which you can link to social media, blogs, and other websites to attract more attention for your books

- Features in the Smashwords store that will expose like category searches, best-seller lists, ratings, "People who recently purchased this book also purchased these books," and "People who recently viewed this author also viewed these authors"

- A flexible sampling system that allows readers to sample up to 50 percent of your book before buying it

- A coupon generation program that lets you send free e-books to reviewers, reward visitors to your blog or forum, or offer free e-books along with print versions of your book

- Automatic enrollment in the Smashwords Affiliate Marketing Program that gives sales commissions to third-party websites, blogs, and affiliate marketers who link to and promote your books

- Smashwords Satellites are more than 30 specialized micro-sites where readers can browse Smashwords e-books by category and topic. (See **www.smashwords.com/labs**)

Publishing with Google eBooks

In December 2010, Google launched its own e-book retail outlet, Google eBooks (**http://books.google.com/ebooks**). With a Google eBook account, readers can purchase an e-book from any e-retailer and be able to download and read it on any type of e-reading device.

To publish through Google eBooks, you must hold the copyright to your book; you cannot publish someone else's book. You can sell your book through Google eBooks if you have a bank account in Australia, Canada, the UK, or the U.S., and only customers with accounts in these countries can buy books. More countries could be eligible in the future.

Once your book is in the Google eBooks database, every word in the text becomes searchable by the Google search engine. Although Google eBooks currently sells only in English-speaking countries, Google Books accepts books in all languages. Books in English, French, Italian, German, Spanish, Dutch, Portuguese, Chinese (simplified), Chinese (traditional), Japanese, Korean, and Russian are completely searchable.

Google eBooks does not accept:

- Incomplete or partial works

- Spam and malware, including content containing links to or promoting the sale of commercial products or soliciting for network marketing. If more than 20 percent of your content is duplicated elsewhere in Google eBooks, your book could be removed.

- Incitement to violence or terrorism, books that threaten to cause serious physical injury or death to an individual or group, and books containing extremely graphic violence

- Content that promotes hate, violence, or genocide toward any identifiable or protected group or individual

- Pedophilia or child pornography

Sexually explicit text and suggestive nudity are permitted as long as they are not made accessible to children. This is accomplished by setting a price of at least $1 (a valid credit card is required for all purchases) and by not allowing any sampling or previews. Graphic sexual images and content that drives traffic to pornography sites are not permitted.

Uploading your book

You can publish on Google eBooks by joining the Google Partners Program (**http://books.google.com/partner/signon**) and uploading a PDF or EPUB file or by mailing a printed copy of your book to Google to be physically scanned. The book will not be returned to you. If you have a PDF and an EPUB version, Google recommends uploading both to make your e-book compatible with more e-reading devices.

To upload your manuscript:

1. Sign in to your Google Books account.

2. Click "Add/Update Books."

3. Click "Upload/Ship Books."

4. Click "Launch Google Uploader."

5. Drag your files from your computer to the "Uploader" window, or browse for them using the "Add Books" button. Save all the files associated with a single ISBN number, such as document files and cover images, in one folder and drag the entire folder into the "Uploader."

6. Add your book information, including ISBN, title, and other preview settings. The "Uploader" will extract metadata from the book files, but fill in any empty blanks.

7. Click the "Upload Files" button to begin the upload.

8. Wait for the upload to complete.

An "Express Live" feature allows you to use the same default settings for all books you upload. You can edit the settings for individual books later.

ISBNs

An ISBN is not required for a Google e-book, but it will be necessary if the book is going to be sold through all the sales channels, including Google eBooks retailers. If your e-book already has ISBNs, use the ISBN from your EPUB version. Follow instructions on Google eBooks for naming your book files with your ISBN number.

If you do not have an ISBN for your e-book, submit it as a non-ISBN title, and it will be assigned a Google-specific ISBN. You can opt out of the Google-specific ISBN by following the instructions in Google eBooks support.

DRM

If Google eBooks sells an e-book published through another publisher, such as Amazon, it administers the DRM in the original document. Google supports Adobe Content Server 4 as its current provider of an industry-standard digital rights management (DRM) solution for downloaded files. You can add DRM management when you upload your book.

Opting out of DRM makes your e-book more accessible for your readers. Google automatically disables cut, copy, save, and print features on the pages of a non-DRM e-book (you might be able to alter these settings in the future). When DRM is enabled, you can go in and allow copying, saving, and printing for all or part of your book.

Paid ad revenue from Google Books Preview Program

As part of the Google Partners Program, you earn revenue from the paid ads displayed alongside previews of your book in Google eBooks. When someone types keywords from your book into the Google search engine, your book preview page appears as one of the search results. If the person clicks on the link to your preview page, you will earn a commission from the Google ads displayed on that page. You control how much of your book, from 20 percent to 100 percent, is made available to readers of your book preview each month. On the preview page for your book, Google includes links to major e-book retailers where your book is sold, plus a "Buy This Book" link to your author website. The "Buy This Book" link must go directly to the title of your book on your website; it cannot go to a third-party affiliate.

You can enroll your book in the Google Books Preview Program even if you do not sell the book through Google eBooks. Follow the instructions for uploading your book to Google eBooks. To participate in the Preview Program you must enter your bank account information. You will be paid at the end of each month if your books have earned more than $100 in ad revenues. Otherwise, you will receive payment after your books have accumulated $100 in ad revenues. You are not allowed to click on the ads appearing on your book pages or to use any kind of mechanical robot to inflate pay-per-click revenues. You may not ask your readers to click on the ads on your preview page.

Selling your book through Google eBooks

To sell your book through Google eBooks, you must first upload it to the Google Books Preview Program. Once it is active in the Preview Program, go to the "Manage eBooks" page in your Partner Programs account. Click on the pencil icon to edit this book's settings, check the box labeled "Enable Google eBooks sales for this title," and save. A "+" in the Participation column indicates your book is available for sale through Google eBooks.

The "eBook Type" column tells you whether the book is available as reflowable text (text only), as a PDF (page images only), or as both reflowable text and a PDF (page images and text). If you uploaded a PDF but your book is "text only," or you uploaded an EPUB and the column says "page images only," it means that the quality of the file you uploaded was poor, and it cannot be used. Create a new PDF file or use Epubcheck (**http:// code.google.com/p/epubcheck**) to find and correct errors in your EPUB file and upload again. "No Files" means you have not yet uploaded files or that they are of poor quality and cannot be used.

Payment for your Google eBook sales goes to the same bank account you registered for the Google Book Preview Program.

Pricing

You can recommend a specified retail list price for your e-book or set the price as a percentage of the lowest price for the print version of your book. The price of your e-book should never exceed the price of any print version of your book. If no price is recommended, Google automatically will set a default price of 80 percent of the price of the print version of your book (if there is one on the market). You also can set a "Bundled Price" if your e-book and print book are sold together.

If you have enrolled a paperback print version and a more expensive hardback print version of your book in Google Books, you will have to delete the hardcover version so that your e-book will be priced competitively based on the cheaper paperback.

You can set a default price that is applied automatically to all your e-book titles when they are uploaded and edit prices for individual books later on.

Once a book is uploaded, you can edit the prices for individual countries and territories. Local laws in some territories require that sales tax be collected. If you select the "Tax exclusive" setting for a territory, Google automatically will calculate sales tax for that territory and add it to the price charged to the customer. If sales tax is included in your list price for a particular territory, select "Tax inclusive" and enter the tax rate you are using as a percentage. The tax amount will be subtracted from the price before your revenue share is calculated.

Promotion on Google books

The most effective marketing feature of Google books is its search feature. Once your book is uploaded, its contents become fully searchable by the Google search engine. This leads people to your books even when they are only searching online for information about a particular topic. You can add these search features and Google Book Previews to your author website.

Sign up for Google Analytics, and you will be able to generate reports showing how people find your books on the Internet and what links they follow to reach your website. This information can help you discover new target markets and improve your metadata to attract more Web traffic.

Chapter 10

Troubleshooting Your E-book — Solutions to Common Problems

The automated technologies that allow you to upload your own manuscript to an e-book publisher and publish it free are truly marvelous. The initial excitement of publishing your e-book may wear thin, however, when you look at it in an e-reader and discover blank pages, text drifting off the side of the page, images appearing randomly here and there, overlapping lines of text, and glaringly ugly fonts. Readers who purchase your book and then find it difficult to read are not likely to buy your future books, could dismiss you forever as a novice and an amateur, and even might express their displeasure publicly with a critical or sarcastic review.

Formatting errors, combined with the idiosyncrasies of various e-reading software programs, cause all of these glitches and aberrations. For this reason, check your e-book before or immediately after publication in a variety of e-reading programs. Invest the time to go through your manuscript thoroughly, and imagine you are experiencing your e-book as a first-time reader. If you detect errors, reformat your manuscript, and republish it. Depending on your e-publisher, the new, improved version will appear online in a few minutes or hours. Remember that you are competing with authors whose publishing companies have invested thousands of dollars to produce professionally formatted e-books that appear beautifully on e-reading devices without any glitches.

When you upload a manuscript to Kindle or NOOK Press, a preview feature allows you to see how your e-book will look in the NOOK or Kindle e-readers before you publish. Review your e-book carefully and patiently in the preview several times before you publish it. You will be able to correct errors and make sure your book is perfect when it goes live for the first time.

If you are publishing with Smashwords or another distributor that supplies multiple formats for a variety of e-readers, or if you are selling your book as a PDF or RTF file directly from your own website, the only way to check it is by looking at it live. If you have an HTML version of your book, open it in your Web browser. Major problems will be easy to spot, and you might be able to locate the problem code in the HTML file and delete or correct it.

You probably do not own 16 different e-reading devices, cell phones, and tablets with which to view your e-book, but you can download the e-reading software for various devices onto your computer. The following free downloads will allow you to see how your book looks in a variety of e-reading devices:

Adobe Digital Editions

(www.adobe.com/products/digitaleditions)

PDF, EPUB, and XHTML

Supports a variety of e-reading devices, including Sony Reader, Acer LumiRead, NOOK, Kobo, PocketBook, and Android apps

Available in English, French, German, Italian, Spanish, Dutch, Brazilian Portuguese, Japanese, Korean, Chinese Simplified, and Chinese Traditional

Kindle for PC

(www.amazon.com/gp/feature.html/ref=kcp_pc_mkt_lnd? docId=1000426311)

Kindle for MAC

(www.amazon.com/gp/feature.html/ref=kcp_mac_mkt_lnd? docId=1000464931)

Free downloads that allow you to read Kindle books and MOBI format on your computer.

NOOK for PC

(www.barnesandnoble.com/u/nook-for-pc/379002322)

Ask friends who own various types of e-reading devices to be your beta readers and give them a free copy of your book in exchange for their feedback on their reading experiences.

How to Fix Common E-Book Formatting Problems

When you discover that your e-book does not look right in an e-reading device, go back to the formatting instructions supplied by your e-publisher, and follow them carefully to reformat your manuscript and republish it.

It might take several tries to find the problem. Sometimes formatting errors are hidden deep within a document. Look for helpful suggestions on your e-publisher's user forums and customer support pages. Solutions to some common problems are suggested below.

I do not have a typed copy of my book

You might have only a print version of an old family memoir or a book you published 20 years ago, and now you want to publish it as an e-book. You have two options: retype the entire manuscript by hand or use a book scanning service to convert your print book to a word-processing file. Commercial scanning services like BlueLeaf Book Scanning (**www.blueleaf-book-scanning.com**), Bound Book Scanning (**http://boundbookscanning.com**), and CSP Book Scanning Services (**www.cspdocscan.com**) will scan your book and convert it with text-recognition software for as little as $15. Many languages are available. Mail in your book, and you will be able to download a typed copy within four to five business days. Destructive book scanning, in which the book is cut from its binding, is less expensive. If your print book is valuable and you want to preserve it, opt for nondestructive scanning using overhead scanners. Some companies will convert your book into a variety of e-book formats. The resulting manuscript is not ready for e-publication until you have reviewed it carefully for typing errors and formatting. Text recognition software is not perfect — it may misread certain combinations of letters.

If you have published in print previously with a POD service, you might have only the PDF manuscript prepared for you by a book layout artist. If possible, ask the person who created the PDF for you to give you a text version of your manuscript that you can open in your word processor. If this is not possible, a number of inexpensive software products convert PDF documents to word processing files. Recosoft (**www.recosoft.com**) and SolidDocuments (**www.soliddocuments.com**) offer free trials of software that opens PDF documents in Word or lets you scan text documents into Word.

Lines of text overlap each other

This is probably a line-spacing error, and it is likely to occur when a document was created in another word processing program such as Open Office and did not convert properly into Microsoft Word. Overlapping lines can occur when the "Line Spacing" settings in the "Paragraph Setup" specify a specific line size. These specific size settings override the e-reader's native settings and cause lines of text to overlap. Examine the formatting of your document for places where the paragraph settings may have changed. Remove these changes, and make sure the entire document has a single paragraph format.

If you are working in Word, highlight the entire manuscript and open the "Paragraph" dialog box (in Word 2007, click the little arrow in the bottom right corner of the "Paragraph" section on the "Home" menu). On the "Indents and Spacing" tab, under "Spacing," make sure the line spacing is single and no value is specified for "At."

If this does not solve the problem, it may be necessary to use Microsoft Notepad or Wordpad to strip all the formatting, as described below, and reformat your document.

Text bleeds off the side of the page

This is often caused by improper margin settings or by indents that are set beyond the margins of your document. Check your margin and indent settings by activating the ruler bar across the top of your word processor. Indents should be set to "0." You can accomplish this by dragging the tabs on the ruler bar to "0" or by altering the "Paragraph" settings in Microsoft Word.

Images appear randomly instead of in the text where they belong

Images were not anchored to text during formatting. If you are formatting in Microsoft Word, you can anchor an image by right-clicking on it with your mouse and selecting "Format Picture," "Layout," and "In Line With Text." Save the change, then highlight the image, and center it. If you formatted your manuscript with Open Office, image settings automatically default to "floating," and you must manually anchor each one. Right-click on each image, and select "Anchor — As Character." Then use the "Center" button to center the image on the page.

Images are cut off on the sides, or only part of an image is showing

This can happen, particularly on the screens of smaller e-reading devices, if the image is so large that it fills a manuscript page from one margin to the other or if the image extends beyond the margin of the page. Images work best if they are less than 500 pixels wide. Use a photo-editing tool to shrink the size of your images.

Images also can be pushed out of position if you are using paragraphs with first-line indents and you forget to remove the first-line indent before an image.

There are blank pages in the e-book

The cause is often too many hard returns in your manuscript. When formatting your manuscript for e-publishing, use the "Enter" key to create a hard return only at the end of each paragraph, unless you are specially formatting poetry, recipes, or lesson materials. Using the "Enter" key more than two times causes some e-reading devices to display blank pages. Other e-reading devices, including Kindle and iPad, add spaces of their own after each paragraph, creating large blank areas. When the "Show/Hide" feature is turned on in Microsoft Word, each hard return is represented by a ¶ (known as a "pilcrow").

I have tried and tried and I cannot find the formatting errors

A manuscript that has been imported from another file format or that has been worked on using multiple word processing programs sometimes contains hidden formatting that causes problems in e-reading devices. The problem might not be obvious when you examine your manuscript, or you might have so many errors that it seems impossible to fix all of them. The best solution is to strip all the formatting out of the document and make a completely fresh start.

Microsoft has two programs, Notepad and WordPad, that strip a document down to bare text. Simply highlight the entire document, copy it, and paste it into a Notepad or WordPad screen. Close Microsoft Word, re-open it, and open a blank, new document. Highlight the entire text in your WordPad or Notepad screen, and paste it into the new Microsoft Word document. You can create a hot key, a macro that clears all the formatting in a document with a single keystroke, by installing a software program such as Pure Text (**www.stevemiller.net/puretext**).

To remove formatting from a portion of your text in Microsoft Word if you are on a PC, highlight the text, and press the "Control" key and spacebar simultaneously. If you are on a Mac, highlight the text, then go up to the formatting box in the toolbars at the top of the page. You also can click "Format," then "Style." From the drop-down menus, choose "Clear Formatting."

My book is mostly photographs and is not displaying well as an e-book

Books such as coffee table books or illustrated children's books composed primarily of images or photos might never look good in EPUB or AZW formats. It might be necessary to publish these books only as PDFs, which will limit your readership somewhat but preserve the appearance and arrangement of your graphics. NOOK Color, Kindle Fire, and many tablet e-reading devices have the capability to display PDF books, and the newest EPUB and Kindle formats accommodate many PDF features.

Question marks or blank boxes are popping up in my e-book

Symbols and characters that are not supported by your e-book file format, such as the copyright symbol or characters from a foreign language, cause these. Avoid using unusual characters or symbols in your text. If a symbol is essential, insert it as a small graphic instead of text.

Chapter 11

Promoting and Selling Your E-Book

The weeks and months of writing, reviewing, editing, and proofreading and the pains you have taken to format your e-book and upload it to e-publishing retail sites are only the first step. To succeed, you need to sell e-books — lots of them. Your e-book is out there, but no one is going to buy it if they do not know about it. Many good books fall off the radar soon after they are released because not enough is done to make readers aware of their existence.

You are competing for readers' attention with millions of other e-writers, including well-known authors, celebrities, journalists, professors, motivational speakers, and indie bloggers. If you are satisfied with merely seeing your name on the cover of an e-book, stop here. However, if you hope to earn an income from your book or if you want to become a recognized author, hard work lies ahead. You need a plan to publicize and market yourself, your book, your ideas, and your future work.

In the days before e-publishing and POD, a writer had to invest several thousand dollars to self-publish a book. To recover this financial investment, authors were prepared to hit the road and visit independent bookstores, arrange public appearances and book signings, and purchase ads in newspapers and magazines. On the other hand, self-publishing e-books requires little investment apart from your time and energy. The Internet offers a vast audience of potential readers — the challenge is to capture their interest and inspire them to recommend your book to hundreds of other readers.

The money you spend to promote your e-book is a business investment, one that you expect to bring in a profit. Your potential market and your plans for the book should determine the size of your budget. If you want to sell hundreds of thousands of copies of your e-book to a broad-market audience, expect to spend thousands of dollars promoting it. An e-book for a niche market might have a much smaller budget. You can take advantage of many free opportunities to publicize your e-book, but even these methods require a good website, eye-catching graphics, know-how, and hours of your time.

When you are spending money to promote your book, think about how to spend that money effectively. For example, paid advertising of any kind is expensive, and most ads are seen by only a tiny percentage of your target audience. A professional website design for your author page, however, is a worthwhile investment that will anchor your marketing efforts for a long time. Sending out a hundred free e-books to reviewers costs almost nothing except the time to locate their email addresses and write a message; a single book review in an indie magazine, online journal, or book blog puts you in front of hundreds of book lovers. TV and radio interviews and direct encounters with readers at public events such as conventions are more likely to attract serious interest than an impersonal paid ad. Depending on the nature of your e-book, you have numerous ways to stretch your marketing budget and get more for your money.

E-books are Eternal

When a new print book is released, it is shipped to bookstores where it is displayed on store shelves and sometimes aggressively promoted with posters and displays at the front of the store. After a few weeks have passed and the publicity campaign has died down, it is relegated to a shelf at the back, and eventually, unsold copies are returned to the publisher to be destroyed. After that, interested readers might not find it while browsing through the store and probably will have to order it online.

A new e-book, in contrast, starts out slowly and gathers momentum as readers recommend it to each other. The e-book stays on the shelf permanently, and each reader that navigates to it and buys it adds to its reputation through ranking lists and Internet search engine traffic. An e-book can continue to generate sales year after year. Each new e-book you publish directs more attention to your previous works. Sales can spike at any time when you are interviewed on the radio, attract publicity in the media, or participate in a public event.

E-books require two kinds of marketing strategies: an initial campaign to get readers interested, and a steady, on-going effort to build and maintain the book's reputation.

Your "First Readers"

While you are still in the earliest stages of writing your book, be thinking about how you are going to sell it. Who is going to read your book, and how are you going to reach them?

Your "first readers" are the first people who take the time to read your book all the way through. First readers are likely to be people who read your book because they are interested in you — friends, family, classmates, co-workers, colleagues, members of your writers' group, members of your clubs and associations. If they are impressed by your book, they are likely to recommend it to their friends or colleagues, who will recommend it to several other people, and so on.

Tell everyone you know that you are about to publish an e-book. When the book becomes available online, send out emails and post announcements on social media. Consider giving friends and associates free copies of your e-book to read, and ask for their feedback. The more people who read your book, the more its reputation will spread to people who want to buy it.

Interacting with Your Readers

Many readers of e-books like to feel personally involved with authors. The most successful e-authors take e-publishing seriously and devote much time to interacting with their audiences. To see how best-selling e-book authors interact with their fans, visit the blogs of Amanda Hocking (**http://amandahocking. blogspot.com**), literary agent Rachelle Gardner (**www.rachellegardner. com**), J.A. Konrath (**http://jakonrath.blogspot.com**) and John Locke (**http://lethalbooks.com**). Some authors even invite their readers to make suggestions about their characters and plots. Authors offer fans that visit their sites additional materials, free excerpts of new books, and other perks.

Strategies for Marketing Your E-book

Marketing yourself on the Internet is not the same as marketing a product sold in retail stores. Browsing on the Internet is an intimate, personal experience. Buyers of e-books know they are important. They believe they have input to the products they buy and that their opinions are respected. Many e-book buyers enjoy "discovering" new books and authors and recommending them to their friends and followers. Online communities form around every imaginable interest. Writing is no longer the sole domain of authors — anyone can write a review, comment, or opinion and post it on a blog or online forum. Readers can "rate" a book with a click of a mouse and "like" or "dislike" it on social networking sites; when readers see that a particular book is attracting a lot of attention, they want to look at it, too. Viral marketing, where readers take over the marketing of your book by promoting it to each other, is every writer's ambition. Obscure people and events suddenly gain worldwide notoriety when they become popular with the millions who spend hours every week looking through YouTube or Facebook.

E-authors employ a variety of strategies to establish their presence on the Internet and in the reading community. Some establish themselves as authorities by writing informative blog posts or contributing regular news articles to online journals. Others create entire cultures around their main characters or their genres. Many have learned to employ social media as a powerful e-marketing tool. As you develop your marketing strategy, your success will be determined by how much of yourself you invest in it. Sincerity and genuine commitment to your writing engage readers and inspire them to spread the word about your e-book to others.

Some of the following strategies can be implemented in a few minutes; others only can be accomplished over a period of days or weeks. Maintain a consistent attitude, and do not lose sight of your long-term goals. As you work on these strategies, you will come up with many good ideas and discover new marketing opportunities.

Make a list of at least ten actions you are going to take to market your e-book. Implement the simple ones first and create a schedule for long-term activities. Set aside some time every week for marketing activities.

Price to sell

The lower you price your book, in theory, the better its chances of selling. Pricing your book too high will discourage potential readers from buying it. Top-selling e-authors sell their books for $0.99 to $2.99. You can make more money by selling thousands of books at $0.99 each than by selling two dozen books for $8.99 each. The more books you sell, the larger your following and the greater the market for your next book.

Start low, and then adjust upwards when you develop a successful sales strategy. However, pricing above $9.99 is not recommended for a typical novel-length work. Price a book available in paperback from $2.99 to $7.99. If your book is only available as an e-book, use discretion when pricing. At the same time, your price should reflect the quality of your book and the investment you made in writing and producing it. Content that is highly technical or graphics-heavy, requires a lot of research, or for which you have to pay contributors demands a higher price.

Pricing strategies

Here are some common pricing strategies for e-books:

Set a low introductory price

Some authors start by pricing their e-books at 99 cents and raise the price as the title gains in popularity — and sales. Others try creative ways to attract buyers, such as donating a portion of the profits to a charity.

Sell low-priced excerpts

To encourage sales of longer works, excerpt stand-alone information and price it lower. This tidbit of information is a teaser that will encourage people to buy the work in its entirety. If yours is a nonfiction work, excerpt some particularly helpful or little-known information from the book. If it is a memoir, novel, or other fictional work, excerpt a high-interest portion such as a point where the action escalates or another highlight from the book. Whatever people read in the excerpt should make them want to read the rest of the work. Excerpts often are priced in e-book stores from 99 cents to $2.49 and are generally article-length, from one to five pages.

E-book Sales and Your Taxes

When you earn income by writing and publishing e-books, you are self-employed, and you must report your income from book sales to the IRS as taxable income. Failing to report income amounts to tax evasion, and tax evasion can incur severe penalties and fines. Self-employment carries other tax obligations, including payment of Social Security and Medicare tax. On the other hand, as a self-employed individual, you can deduct business expenses from your taxable income and even might be able to deduct part of the cost of maintaining your home, if a portion of it is set aside as a dedicated business office. If you do not want to run afoul of the IRS, and you want to claim as many legitimate tax deductions as you can, you need to understand self-employment taxes. You can find extensive tax information on the IRS website (**www.irs.gov**), and many websites and blogs offer tax tips for freelance writers.

Do not wait until March of next year, when you start filling out your tax return, to start adding up receipts and calculating your profit or loss. The sooner you set up an organized recordkeeping system, the more accurate those records will be and the more you will be able to claim in legitimate deductions. Keep all receipts for office supplies, computer equipment, computer software, postage, and anything else you buy specifically for your writing and e-publishing activities. Keep accurate records of payments for graphic artists, editing and formatting services, paid advertising or marketing services, and download and save copies of statements and bank records. Records and receipts must be kept for at least seven years in case the IRS selects you for an audit or questions the information on your tax return.

Federal income taxes are not the only potential pitfall. Your state and even your city may require you to pay income tax. If you sell hard copies of your book or book-related merchandise online, some state governments require you to pay sales tax on retail sales. Major retail channels automatically will charge and deduct sales tax when it is owed, but if you are selling directly from your website, you are responsible for learning about your state's sales tax policies and obtaining a state tax ID. Local jurisdictions might require you to pay a business tax or purchase a business license. Because your first book is only the beginning of your writing career, it is a good idea to learn as much as you can while you are getting started to avoid making serious mistakes that could cost you later.

Serialize your title

If you have a long-form work, consider serializing it, or breaking it up into smaller sections and selling those separately from one another. Your work does not have to be fiction to be serialized, but it should be long enough to be broken up into smaller subsections. Consider the possibilities of serializing a memoir or a nonfiction book. Each chapter should stand on its own and end in a manner that generates interest for whatever comes next. A number of notable works were first published this way, including many of Charles Dickens' novels and *The Diary of Bridget Jones.*

You can complete the work in its entirety and then begin serializing it or write it as you go. Once your e-book has been serialized from start to finish, you can publish it as a single volume. Serialization generates interest in your work; a person who reads the first few chapters and is interested enough to want to read more will eagerly anticipate the next installment. If your work is good enough, word-of-mouth will bring in new readers.

Many serial writers create an online community centered on a blog or website and engage their readers by communicating with them regularly.

Sell your book through multiple channels

Offer your book for sale through Kindle, Barnes & Noble, indie retail sites, iPhone apps, affiliate book retailers, and your own websites and blogs. The more exposure you have on the Internet, and the more links to your book and author pages, the more likely people are to come across your book when they do a search. Ask your friends which websites they go to for their e-books. Many readers have one or two favorite e-stores where they look for books — make sure your book is there to be found.

Remove all barriers

In any type of e-commerce, potential buyers can be discouraged from buying at any point in the process if they receive a bad first impression, cannot access information about your product, or encounter difficulty while making a payment. A poorly designed book cover, typos and clichés in your book copy, a sample that takes too long to download, a payment system that excludes a major credit card, an incompatible format, text that appears incorrectly in the e-reader screen, frustration with navigating through the book — any of these could cause a reader to bypass your e-book in favor of another author. DRM can be a barrier if it prevents your readers from downloading or sharing your books.

Think about your readers' experience from search engine through your final chapter and beyond, and eliminate any possible barrier to buying and enjoying your book. Follow the suggestions earlier in this book to produce a beautiful e-book of the best quality.

Though Kindle and NOOK dominate in the U.S., readers use many types of e-reading devices. Your audience includes everyone who speaks English. Make your book available in as many formats for as many types of e-reading devices as possible.

From time to time, look at your book with different e-readers or e-reading software to see what your readers are experiencing. Pay attention to comments or feedback that indicate any kind of displeasure or difficulty, and try to find the source of the problem. If your book is listed in several retail outlets, and one of them is producing no sales, you could have a problem with your format or with your listing for that retailer. Either readers cannot find your listing, or they are having difficulty downloading your book.

Learn from other e-authors. Look at how other authors in your genre present their e-books in retail stores. Buy some books, and download them to see what kind of experience they offer. If you like a particular feature, your readers would probably like it, too.

Make your book easy to find

Use keywords related to the content of your book in the title, subtitle, front matter, and book copy, as well as on your author profiles. Always think about how your readers will find you. For nonfiction books, the title should contain a clear reference to the topic: *Trading Gold.* Add more detail in the subtitle: *How to Get Rich Buying and Selling Gold and Precious Metals.* For fiction books, clearly identify your genre when creating a book listing, book page, or author page. Your book copy should contain your genre and the names of major characters.

Most search engine results display the first few words of a book description. The lead-in sentences of your book copy or book description should clearly identify the nature of your book:

"Angel thought she had everything under control, until the handsome stranger walked through her front door…"

"For 10,000 years the Atrons have ruled the universe unchallenged. Now, a strange event on a tiny, distant planet threatens to…"

"Here, at last, are the answers parents have been waiting for…"

If you write a series of e-books, maintain a theme such as similar titles and covers, so readers instantly identify the book as yours.

Sampling

Mimicking the experience of a reader browsing through the shelves of a bookstore, most e-book retailers offer free samples of content from each book. Offering free chapters, sample excerpts, and condensed versions of your e-book entices readers to pay for the entire book. For example, Kindle offers the first chapter of each book free. Some stores offer the first 15 percent of a book as a sample, and a few offer as much as 50 percent and let you decide how much of your book to make available free.

Make it clear that only a portion of the book is free; otherwise, frustrated readers might give you negative reviews when they find they cannot see the entire book.

Remember not to fill the front of your e-book with large graphics, blank pages, long introductions, and other material that might take up too much of a 15-percent sample. You want the reader to be able to read enough of your book to get hooked.

Free books

Most successful e-book authors offer at least one of their titles free. A free book allows readers to become acquainted with your characters and your writing style; if they enjoy the free book, they will want to buy your other books.

You also can offer a limited number of e-books free as a promotion or send free copies of your e-book to reviewers and journalists. Most e-publishers have a coupon program that generates a promotional code for free or discounted copies of your book.

Offer free copies to the first 25 people that respond to a blog post or a tweet.

Many owners of e-readers look for free e-books on websites such as:

- Free-Online-Novels.com
  (**http://free-online-novels.com/submissions.html**)
- EnglishNovels.net (**http://www.englishnovels.net**)
- Getfreeebooks (**www.getfreeebooks.com**).

Offering a free title will get you exposure on these sites to thousands of booklovers that are actively searching for a new read. Free books also will gain you additional exposure on your book retailer website as part of its free book promotions.

Build links to your book

One of the elements that raises the status of your book in Internet search engines is the number of times people link to and visit your book and author pages. Include a link to your book page wherever you can — in your email signature, social media pages, blog posts, websites, and anywhere that you have a personal or an author profile. Make it easy for your readers to pass on the link to your book page. For example, if you send out a tweet with a blurb or a quote from your book, include a link to your book page. Anyone who retweets will pass on the link to others. Make your email announcements interesting so recipients will forward them, and be sure to feature the link to your book page prominently in the first part of the email.

Maximize tags and metadata

Metadata is additional information about your book that is tucked into HTML code and added to Web page descriptions. It can include keywords and information about your genre, book topic, and publication dates. Metadata is used to organize books on the virtual bookshelves of online retailers, just as books in a physical bookstore are organized by category and subject. Metadata tags are the basis for "people who read this book also enjoyed these books" features. Metadata also helps site searches and search engines to locate your book when someone types certain words into the search box. Accurate metadata is essential when your potential readers are searching for you among millions of e-books.

Do not overlook the places where you are asked to enter "tags" or select categories when uploading your book. Choose words that closely match your book contents, and enter your genre or category as the first keyword or tag. Use first name-last name in the blank for "author's name." A tag can contain two or more words; think of the words your readers will use to search for your topic.

All e-book retail stores do not search metadata in the same way. If your e-book is showing up under a strange category name, check the metadata by adding it to a library in Calibre (**http://calibre-ebook.com**) and then clicking on "Edit Metadata." Find the source of the problem, and then go to your e-book publisher and correct your metadata.

Write good book copy

Your book copy is a concise, well-written paragraph explaining what your e-book is about and how the reader will benefit from reading it. It is the first paragraph of text on your e-book's Web pages, and sometimes the first few sentences appear alongside your cover image and title in book retailer listings. The book copy converts a potential reader's casual curiosity into a sale. You have just a few seconds to capture a reader's interest.

Start with a strong headline that immediately captures the reader's attention. Follow that with a "hook," a sentence that entices the reader into reading more. For example, "Earn a million dollars in one year," or, "For 27 years, she had never ventured more than two blocks from her front door…" Follow that with a list of what the reader will learn by reading a nonfiction book or a succinct setup of the plot for a fiction book. End with a call to action — motivate the reader to buy your book. The book copy also can contain one or two sentences promoting you as the author.

Take time to craft a paragraph that not only describes the content of your book but also conveys the essence of your genre. A book copy for a fast-paced detective story should contain two or three intriguing details that define the book; for a romance, the book copy should hint at the heroine's dilemma. A book copy for a business book should bristle with confidence and authority.

Many writers have difficulty writing a strong book copy. If you are one of them, ask another writer to help you, or hire a copywriter to write it for you.

Blurbs, if you have them, should follow the book copy. A blurb is a short endorsement of you or your book taken from a book review or made by a well-known person or one who has a professional title. Give the speaker's name and title after each comment. You can obtain endorsements by asking people to review your book or sample chapters, and then ask for written permission to put their testimonials on your cover. If someone introduces you publicly at a lecture or a professional gathering, ask if you can quote him or her in your book. Most prominent people like to have their names published. If you belong to a writer's group or a professional association, you can ask fellow members for endorsements. Never pay anyone for an endorsement, or it will have no value.

Make the most of your retail listings

Every retail outlet offers numerous opportunities to promote your book(s). Make the most of the fact that your e-book is listed in a place where millions of people go to look for books. Each listing must be cultivated carefully because every e-book you sell increases your ranking in that retail outlet. It is a snowball effect — the more books you sell, the more readers you attract. For each of your retail outlets:

- Follow instructions to format your book so that it displays well, and upload a good cover image.

- Write a good book description.

- Enter relevant tags and metadata.

- Take time to create a good author page, including links to your social media profiles.

- Invite readers to post reviews.

- Participate in the retailer's promotions by offering free books, generous sampling, and coupons.

- Write reviews for other authors' books, and include a link to your author page in the signature.

Read the retailer's user forums and pick up tips from other authors on how to promote your book on the site.

Exploit social media as much as you can

Use Facebook, Twitter, LinkedIn, and writers' communities to interact with potential readers. Post comments and make appearances on the websites and forums of online communities that might be interested in your e-book. For example, if your book is about raising children, participate in parenting forums and mommy websites. If you write about food or travel, post frequent comments on recipe or travel sites. Update your author profiles often, and add new material to your social pages regularly.

Solicit book reviews

Book reviews are (almost) free publicity. They also can be powerful marketing tools. You will find it difficult to get your self-published e-book reviewed by a newspaper or website, but it is worth trying. Excerpts from reviews provided before the book's release can be used as blurbs (the quoted promotional copy that appears in book descriptions or in the front matter, or beginning pages, of books), and on your blog, Amazon Author Page, or personal website.

You can include (positive) review copy with your listing on Amazon, Barnes & Noble, and other retail bookseller websites. Remember that a review is copyrighted material just like any other published printed matter, so use excerpts sparingly and be sure to include proper attribution.

Define your target audience and think about the newspapers, magazines, newsletters, and websites they read. Make a list of publications that might be interested in reviewing your book, and gather email addresses for their book reviewers. Be creative. If yours is a nonfiction book with a historical subject, send review queries to publications that review nonfiction as well as those concerned with the subject matter, such as historical societies and organizations. A mommy website might review a book about nutrition for children, or a church newsletter might be interested in a book about dealing with grief.

Send out review query letters or emails, and email a free copy of your e-book to those who respond positively, rather than blindly emailing copies of your e-book out to publishers and organizations. Some reviewers will not review e-books, POD editions, or self-published works; it is wise to view submission guidelines before sending in your work.

When you email a free e-book to a book reviewer, attach a copy of your press release and a review slip to the email. Book reviewers might do 15 reviews a week and do not have time to read a book completely. For this reason, the book copy and the press release you include with your book are important. The reviewer may use excerpts from them as part of the review. *See Appendix E for a sample review query letter and a sample review slip.*

The Difference Between a Book Critic and a Reviewer

A book critic reads the whole book and provides educated and in-depth commentary.

Some book reviewers might not read the entire book and often will write their reviews based on the press release, book copy, front matter, and from skimming through the book.

Follow up with a nice letter or email to anyone who takes the time to review your book, and let him or her know you appreciate it, even if the review is negative. Be professional, and avoid tongue-in-cheek comments. Remember that anyone who reviews your book has put time into reading it and most likely was not paid for doing so unless they work for a major publication.

Reader reviews serve a different purpose: they are read by other readers, and posted along with your book listings in retail outlets to help people decide whether to buy your book. One or two good reviews greatly increase the likelihood that a shopper will buy your book. However, no one wants to read a review by your grandmother or best friend gushing about what a wonderful book it is and what a great writer you are. Only a thoughtful, interesting review will make people want to read your book. Send free copies of your e-book to members of your writers' group, book club, or online community and invite them to post reviews on retail outlets and book review sites. Be sure to give them links to the places where you would like them to post reviews.

E-Books in the Headlines

Crossover Novelist Uses Crossover Marketing Tactics

In an interview with *Entertainment Weekly*, singer/songwriter Josh Ritter says his debut novel *Bright's Passage* was inspired by an idea for a narrative song. When the book was released in June 2011 by The Dial Press, an imprint of Random House, it received numerous reviews, including a Sunday book review in *The New York Times* by author Stephen King. Random House orchestrated an extensive marketing campaign based on Ritter's fame as a musician, while Ritter, a veteran who began his career selling self-published CDs at open mic nights and live performances, turned to the same tactics musicians use to sell their music. He released a free download of the first chapter for his fans through TopSpin Media (**www.topspinmedia.com**), which collected their email addresses in the process. The link for the download was placed on his website and on NPR's *All Songs Considered*, with a share button so fans could recommend it to each other. He recruited Hollywood friends, family members, and fans to take turns reading the first chapter of the novel for a 20-minute video that was hosted on the website of *Entertainment Weekly*. Another video of him reading from his book during an interview with PBS was posted on YouTube. On his website Ritter sells *Bright's Passage* merchandise, including T-shirts, bookmarks and stickers, just as he sells merchandise tie-ins with his CDs and live performances.

Book review by Stephen King (**www.nytimes.com/2011/07/03/books/review/book-review-brights-passage-by-josh-ritter.html?_r=1**)

Video of friends and family reading the first chapter of Bright's Passage (**http://shelf-life.ew.com/2011/07/14/josh-ritter-brights-passage**)

PBS Interview (**www.pbs.org/newshour/art/blog/2011/07/monday-on-the-newshour-josh-ritter.html**)

YouTube video (**http://www.youtube.com/watch?v=xVUuNlHoa08**)

Create a media portfolio and a promotions file

A media portfolio is a collection of all the materials you use to promote your book and yourself as an author. It includes your book copy, press releases, headshot, author bio, a graphic of your book cover, book reviews and endorsements, videos and book trailers, and press clippings. A well-organized media portfolio saves you hours of time and makes it possible for you to respond almost instantly when someone contacts you. It also helps you maintain a consistent image by using the same headshot and copy on all your author pages, blogs, and websites. As you expand your marketing campaign, you could create several media portfolios for different audiences that promote different aspects of your book. Create a folder on your computer for your media portfolio, with sub-folders for specific marketing campaigns and projects. Your media portfolio should be accessible easily, with a backup copy on a flash drive or online storage. If you are attending a writers' convention or other networking event or appearing in a radio or TV interview, copy your media portfolio onto inexpensive flash drives or CDs that you can hand out to people who want to post information about you on their websites.

Anytime you write something about your book, such as a book description for an online bookseller, file a copy in your media portfolio so you can use it again the next time you need a similar description. Keep a folder of all news articles about you or your book, along with reviews and anything that has been said about you on blogs. Prepare a file you can email quickly to anyone who asks for information about you.

Your promotions file should include contact lists of media and book reviewers to whom you send out press releases and book review queries, along with records of their responses. These lists will be invaluable to you as you pursue your writing career. Develop a media contact list of people who can help you promote your e-books, and develop relationships with them. Keep records of your interactions, and note any personal information they divulge so you can bring it up when you speak to them again.

Set a publication date

Choose a date in the future as your "publication date." It does not have to be the date your e-book first appears for sale online — it is simply a point in time around which you can structure your publicity campaign. You will need to give the publication date in directory listings, and you will mention it in your press releases, on your website and in any announcements you send out. Send out a round of press releases announcing the release of your e-book on that date. Arrange for interviews at local TV and radio stations. Because you are a local resident, you probably will receive some recognition, and you can begin adding links to those videos and recordings to your website and your media portfolio. If appropriate, set your publication date to coincide with a related holiday or event, such as an election or Valentine's Day. Once the publication date has passed, remove references to it from your press releases, and focus on a new angle to promote your book.

Send out press releases

A press release is easy and inexpensive to send out. Press releases can go out whenever you have some kind of news to announce: the release of your book, your appearance at a charity event or conference, or your book's relevance to a current event or social issue. Press releases are the source of 20 to 25 percent of the content in most newspapers and magazines.

Editors always are looking for interesting content to print. Study each publication and tailor your press release to match its tone and style. Do not make a news release sound like advertising copy. Write using a journalistic approach so the text can be inserted directly into a news article. Keep your sentences short (about 23 words) and use clear, down-to-earth language. Start with an attention-grabbing headline and an interesting "hook" in the first sentence. The news release can focus on you, on your book, or on a newsworthy event or situation related to your book, but make sure your book title is mentioned.

Most press releases are one page; if you want to add more material, separate your author bio and attach it as a second press release. Newspapers like to print photographs along with articles; your chances of getting noticed are greater if you provide a good-quality image of yourself, your book cover, or something to do with your topic or include a link where a high-resolution image can be downloaded from your website. *See a sample press release in Appendix E.*

A press release can be sent by email, and many publications have online submission forms. Always copy and paste text from a Word document rather than typing it directly into a submission form, so you can spell check it and keep a record of what you have sent out. Keep your press releases organized. For example, you can give each one a number or a date. On a spreadsheet, note the publication, email address or submission URL, the date, and the number of the press releases you sent.

News release services post announcements and send out press releases to thousands of media outlets, as well as hosting your press releases on their sites. The following sites send out your press releases free:

- I-Newswire (**www.i-newswire.com**)
- PRLog (**www.prlog.org/submit-free-press-release.html**)
- PR.com (**www.pr.com**)

These sites offer additional fee-based PR services, and other news release services like PRNewswire (**www.prnewswire.com**) charge a fee per press release or a monthly subscription fee. Remember how many e-books you will have to sell to cover the cost of these services. It is probably more effective to submit your press release directly to targeted media outlets. If you succeed in creating a buzz about your book in e-book circles and writers' communities, journalists will hear about it.

Schedule a blog tour

Writers of established blogs are often looking for new material to make their blogs more interesting. Use Google Blog Search (**www.google.com/ blogsearch**) or Technorati (**http://technorati.com**) to find blogs that feature authors or pertain to your topic. Contact the blog owner and offer to write a guest post. Make yourself available to answer reader comments for a day or two after the post goes live and participate in any ensuing discussions. Do not blatantly promote your e-book — stick to the blog topic and make your post as interesting as you can. Instead, introduce yourself as the author of your e-book and provide a link to your author page or website.

Advertising

Advertisements are expensive, but some forms of paid advertising can be worthwhile if they are particularly suited to your book.

- Direct marketing — Paid ads in newsletters, direct mail inserts, and order forms placed in catalogs and books can bring good results if they are targeted to people who will be especially interested in your book.

- Email marketing — Purchase a mailing to a targeted email list or create your own mailing list of people who sign up on your website to receive email, e-newsletters, and other updates. Avoid sending spam; unsolicited email should be avoided because it can damage your credibility. You also can get email exposure by purchasing an ad in someone else's online newsletter — for example, if you belong to a professional or trade association that sells advertising in its newsletter.

- Online ads — Paid ads on Amazon.com, other booksellers' websites (such as Powell's Books at **www.powells.com**) and through Google Adwords (see **http://adwords.google.com**) can drive sales if they are targeted carefully with specific keywords. Websites that host online communities of readers or specialize in free and cheap e-books often sell inexpensive ads or offer paid "featured book" programs and cross-promotions with other books of the same genre. Purchase paid advertising for a specific period or number of ads, and track the results to see if the sales results justify the expenditure. Be wary of buying "pay per click" ads because you pay every time someone clicks on the ad. An interesting ad could attract an unexpected number of click-throughs and leave you a big bill with few resulting sales.

Book Publicists

Book publicists are public relations experts who specialize in promoting books. Even authors whose books are published by conventional publishing companies hire book publicists to help them market their books. *Publisher's Weekly* estimates that there are about 200 book publicists in the U.S. A book publicist has established contacts that can get an author interviews on national radio and TV stations and appearances on talk shows. The book publicist also coaches an author for success by identifying qualities of the book and the author's personal life that will make good talking points and attract public attention. An author works with a book publicist for a minimum of six months. These services can be expensive and are beyond the reach of most self-published authors.

You can get professional help with your marketing campaign by hiring a freelance publicist to help you create a marketing plan and media contact list, write press releases and fliers, and arrange public appearances. Freelancers are paid by the hour or by the job, and you can purchase their services as you need them.

Chapter 12

Promoting Yourself

Writers never stop writing. Your first e-book teaches you the mechanics of writing and perfecting a book, formatting skills, and the basics of marketing and promotion. Now you can apply that knowledge to your next e-book and another e-book after that. Each new book adds to your reputation and your catalog and attracts additional readers for your previous books. Your writing becomes more than a hobby and even might lead to a full-time career.

Along with the efforts you make to market your first e-book, you must begin a long-term campaign to market yourself as an author. Readers who like your first book will want to know more about you. The Internet gives them instant access to information and unprecedented opportunities to interact with you. In the age of printed books, fans met authors at book signings, sent them letters through the mail, read about them in magazines and occasionally heard them on the radio or saw them on a TV talk show. Today, a fan can read all about you on your website, post on your blog, sign up for your email newsletter, and follow you on Twitter.

You are not obligated to tell the world everything about yourself, your family background, or your business and leisure activities. Be selective about what you reveal to your readers. Create an online persona that will engage your fans and stick to it. Share information that will resonate and enhance your authority as an author. For example, if you are writing a parenting guide, parents will want to know you are a pediatrician or a child psychologist, or a parent yourself speaking from personal experience. Readers of a book about investing in the stock market will not care whether you have children, unless you are promoting investment as a way to secure your family's future. Instead, they want to know how you gained your experience and what your qualifications are. Young adults do not want to know that the author of their favorite romance series is 65 years old — they would rather hear about her personal life experiences and her pets or perhaps receive information that is useful and interesting for their age group. A writer of science fiction, crime, or fantasy might want to portray himself or herself as someone one step removed from being a main character in the novel.

Building Your Platform

Whether you are marketing your own self-published e-books, pitching your book to an agent or a conventional publisher, or submitting an application for a job, your author "platform" is a major selling point. Your platform is a combination of your public reputation and your résumé or portfolio, all the unique factors that contribute to making readers want to buy your book. A pastor of a megachurch, a TV talk-show host, a politician, a celebrity, or a well-known fitness guru with a large following already has a platform — a large group of interested followers. An author who has published a best seller also has an established platform. As a first-time author, you must build your platform from the ground up by investing time and effort to publicize yourself as well as your e-book. Publishing books is a lifelong career. As soon as you publish your first e-book, be working on your next project(s). A book is only one facet of your career — it can lead you to publish a series of books, create a franchise, become a public speaker, or position yourself as an authority in your field. Building a platform ensures you will always have a ready-made audience for your next endeavor.

Your platform has to be nurtured and cared for over time. It takes almost as much work as writing books and is just as important. Begin by considering what you already have accomplished. Professional and academic credentials are part of your platform if they give you particular authority to write about your subject matter. So, is personal experience — for example, working as a nanny for 20 years, managing a construction company, or taking care of an autistic child. Are you active in a group or association whose members know and respect you? How can you expand on these activities? What can you do to add to your reputation?

Your "platform" is anything you do to make a name for yourself. Book tours, public appearances, speeches, and seminars at which you promote your e-book, and radio and TV interviews all bring you into direct contact with potential readers. Someone who has met you in person or listened to you speak will not forget your name when they see it on the Internet or the listing for your e-book.

The activities you do to build your platform depend on your genre and the type of e-books you publish. The goal is to make yourself widely known to the people interested in reading your book. For fiction writers, those activities involve making as many readers as possible aware of your books and developing a following of loyal fans who cannot wait for the next book to come out. In addition to publicity and marketing campaigns, a fiction writer can build a platform by giving talks and lectures, holding blog tours, and cultivating an online presence. To promote children's e-books, give talks at public libraries — announce them with press releases to local papers and make video recordings to post on your website. A science fiction author can rent a table and talk to fans at science fiction conventions. An author of a book written for a small niche market can focus on establishing a reputation within that market. Every public appearance should be accompanied by media attention and announcements on your website.

A nonfiction author must work on establishing a reputation in his or her field by participating in conferences, contributing articles to journals and newspapers, writing for blogs, and sending out regular email newsletters. A nonfiction e-book, or series of e-books, can become a springboard for a new career.

Radio and Television Interviews

A radio or television interview brings you into intimate contact with potential readers, right in their homes, cars, or workplaces. For a few minutes, you have their full attention. This makes interviews an effective way to promote your book.

Major radio or TV stations want to hear a sample interview or audition video before committing themselves to an interview. Get some practice by seeking interviews on college radio and TV stations, Internet radio stations, or at small local radio stations. Once you have recorded that first interview, you can send the recording along with your other interview requests.

Before contacting a radio station, find out what shows they run and whether any relate to the topic of your book. Start by looking at their websites for their scheduling and programs. Come up with a "hook" that is newsworthy, timely, or informative, or that relates both to current events and to your book or topic. If your book takes place in a certain locale, stations in that area probably will be interested in helping to promote a published work of local interest. Your role on the show will be to entertain listeners, so promote your interesting or unique idea rather than overtly promoting your book. Your book title will be mentioned in the introduction, and you might have a chance to refer to it once or twice, but the topic is what will hold your listeners' attention. Radio interviews sometimes are done over the phone, and they can be live or taped.

Contact local television stations, pitch your idea to them, and if you are traveling to their area, let them know you are on tour and your availability. Once you have notified the local media of your talk, tour, reading, or event, you never know when they will send out a reporter or camera crew, so be prepared. Before contacting any media outlet, learn about its audience and tailor your idea to fit its needs. Targeting a dozen stations selectively is better than blindly sending press releases to hundreds of stations. Address your cover letter to a specific person at each station if possible.

Stay relaxed during the interview. Get plenty of rest the night before, and if you will be appearing on TV or in a video, have clothes picked out ahead of time (no busy patterns). Visit the Internet for tips on radio and television interviews so you have some idea of what to expect. Women should wear makeup a little darker than normal for television and arrive ready for taping. Your personal grooming and overall appearance are important. On air, be yourself, and stay focused on your topic. Be prepared for chitchat and banter, and prepare what you want to say ahead of time. Be flexible, and prepare to work your comments in at a different angle than you have anticipated. You can ask ahead of time if a television station can prepare a chyron (ky-run) for you — a graphic or text caption superimposed at the bottom of a TV screen while you speak. Email the station an attachment of the book cover and information about the book, such as a press release and book copy. During the show, mention where the book can be found online and the time and location of any events or readings. After the taping, send a thank-you note.

Social Media

The Internet gives you access to millions of potential followers, 24 hours a day. An interested reader quickly can look up information about you, your other books, and similar books by other authors. Readers like to know more about the background of a book and to read additional material such as the author's commentary or unpublished sections that were left out of a book. They also enjoy being able to communicate with an author or to participate in a fantasy world based on a book. All of this activity strengthens a reader's loyalty to an author.

Although you have little control over who views your Internet presence or what they do once they are attracted by it, the sheer number of viewers makes it effective. It is worth your while to master the use of social media and take full advantage of it. If you feel you do not have time for social media, hire someone to do it for you. Once your various accounts and profiles are set up, you can manage your social media by scheduling a few hours every week to review and update them. Your Internet presence should be more active when you are leading up to the release of a new book or a public appearance to generate interest and attract Web traffic. At other times, you only might need to write some blog posts and check email.

If you write nonfiction books, you might invest more time in your website and social media: sending out newsletters or Twitter about your topic, hosting an online journal, or posting a series of how-to articles. Remember your purpose, which is to establish and maintain a reputation that will help sell your books, and tailor your social media activities appropriately.

Keep Your Public and Personal Lives Separate

Although your fans like to feel they have a personal connection with you, be careful about what you share on social media. Keep a consistent public image, and use privacy settings to protect personal communication from reaching people who should not be reading them. Avoid using obscenities or disparaging language. When someone receives attention from the media, one of the first places journalists look for information is that person's social media accounts. Everything you say could end up on the front page of a newspaper. Unless your book is about your family life (and even if it is!), do not post photos of your children; doing so could attract unwanted attention and even endanger them.

One of the best things about social media is that it costs you nothing except your time and energy. Yet, if used effectively, it can gain you more exposure to potential readers than thousands of dollars in paid advertising. You can access the millions of people who use social networking sites simply by setting up an account, and in many cases, you are able to direct your efforts straight to the people most likely to be interested in your book.

Social media is also effective for networking and communicating with other authors, agents, journalists, publishing industry professionals, and others who might be interested in your career. These people can act as mentors and advisers, put you in contact with professionals or businesses that offer services you need, or help you land a book or writing deal or a public speaking engagement.

Entire books have been written about exploiting social media, and courses on the subject are taught at universities. By setting up several social media profiles and linking them to each other and to your blogs and websites, you can generate activity on the Internet and attract search engine traffic. The following is a brief overview of major social media sites. By the time you read this book, there might be new trends. The Internet evolves rapidly, so pay attention when you hear about the emergence of something new and different.

Activities like blogging, tweeting, and updating your Facebook pages can take hours of your time. Spend some time familiarizing yourself with the various social media sites, and select the strategy that will be the best fit for your book(s).

Facebook

Any individual can open a Facebook (**www.facebook.com**) account under a personal name or a pen name. Once you set up a Facebook account, you have two pages: your profile and your home page. Your profile contains the information you want the world to see, including an area called a "wall" where you can post brief messages. Your home page contains information that Facebook wants to communicate to you, including news feeds of posts on other Facebook pages to which you are connected.

You can invite other people with Facebook accounts to be your friends ("friend" them). If they accept, you will appear on each other's lists of friends, and your wall posts will appear on each other's Facebook profile pages. Privacy settings control how your information is shared on Facebook; for example, you can create a block list of people who are not allowed to access your site. Because the public will see your Facebook page, it is a good idea to check each person's profile before you accept a "friend" request. If they post profanity or strange comments on your wall, these will appear on your profile.

You can create a Facebook fan page for your book or even a character from your book. The fan page allows you to post comments and information for your fans and allows them to post comments and communicate with each other. You cannot "friend" people from your fan page; they have to find your page and connect to it themselves. You can attract followers to your fan page by linking to it from articles, blogs, and email newsletters. A fan page allows you to post photos of events and links to your books' sales pages. To keep fans coming back, regularly update your fan page with new information, photos, or comments.

Facebook also sells targeted pay-per-click ads displayed to Facebook users. Because you only pay when someone clicks on the ad, it can be an economical way of advertising your book. If you purchase pay-per-click ads, be sure to monitor your account; an intriguing ad might generate more responses, and a higher advertising bill, than you expected.

Facebook also provides an avenue for communicating with your own personal "platform." It currently has more than 750 million users worldwide. Many people who know you probably have Facebook accounts and will be curious about your book. Old high school and college friends, business colleagues, people you meet at conferences and meetings, and relatives will find your page on Facebook and might buy your books or recommend them to others. If you have written a family memoir or a highly specialized book, Facebook is a way to communicate with the people who will be most interested in it.

MySpace

MySpace (**www.myspace.com**) preceded Facebook as a social networking site. In February 2012, it had 25 million users. It has evolved into a popular showcase for independent musicians, but its structure makes it difficult for authors to use it effectively. You will have to decide whether you want to invest additional time in cultivating an online presence on MySpace if you are already active with a Facebook account.

Twitter

Twitter (**www.twitter.com**) allows you to send 140-character text messages (tweets) to everyone who is "following" you. People can sign up to be your followers by clicking a Twitter button placed on your website, Facebook page, blog, and on publishing company author pages. Twitter is free. Your Twitter home page contains a form for typing messages and lists your followers. Your profile page contains information about you and all of your tweeted messages. Twitter can be a good way to remind fans when a new book is coming out or when you are doing a public appearance. A tweet can be forwarded (retweeted) to other peoples' followers, so it can be a good way to take your message viral.

Some fiction writers set up Twitter accounts for characters in their books and send out tweets as though the character were communicating with fans. Nonfiction writers can tweet updated information, helpful tips, or recommendations of recent news articles. Because the 140-character limit makes it difficult to type long URLs in a tweet, use a free online link shortening service such as Bitly (**www.bit.ly**) or Is.gd (**www.is.gd**) — just paste in the URL to get a shortened version you can use in a tweet.

Use Twitter effectively by sending interesting and helpful information. Avoid sending frequent tweets that will annoy people.

LinkedIn

LinkedIn (**www.linkedin.com**) is a social-media networking site for professionals with 120 million users. More formal than Facebook and Twitter, LinkedIn allows you to post a business profile, such as your experience, current positions, memberships, alumni status, awards, and accolades. You can connect with other professionals, send direct messages, and "recommend" or be recommended by others you are affiliated with. LinkedIn can be a valuable resource for freelancers and independent authors, because it puts you in contact with agents, potential collaborators, and other professionals interested in your career.

YouTube

YouTube (**www.youtube.com**) allows anyone to upload a video or a film clip to the Internet, where the whole world can see it at any time. As of February 2012, YouTube had 500 million unique users worldwide every month, with an estimated 92 billion page views per month. According to YouTube, on average more than 400 tweets per minute contain a YouTube link. More than 150 years' worth of YouTube videos are watched every day on Facebook. Startling and unusual videos seem to be the most popular, and when a few people find a video they enjoy, they begin passing the link around until it has been viewed hundreds of thousands of times.

YouTube is the best place to upload your video, lecture, or book trailer because it can be found there easily by anyone searching for your name or the title of your book. You can embed a YouTube video on a website or blog and even in an e-book. YouTube constantly ranks the most popular videos; if your video achieves this stature, even more people will view it.

Make a video of yourself reading an excerpt from your book or of visual images associated with your content. Be careful about using music or song lyrics because copyright infringement can result in your video being blocked. If yours is a nonfiction book, create videos illustrating various aspects of your topic or demonstrating how to do something. You can put links to the YouTube videos in corresponding sections of your e-book.

Upload several videos and create a YouTube Channel. Fans who subscribe to your channel will receive notification every time you upload something new. Keep your fans engaged by regularly adding new content. Increase your visibility by partnering with other authors in your genre. Readers who enjoy one author will want to look at your trailers, too, in hopes of finding new books to read.

Blogs

While you have been researching your book and learning how to publish it, you probably have come across hundreds of interesting blog posts. A good blog establishes you as an authority in your area of interest and enables people to get to know you — or at least get to know your public persona. A good example of an effective blog is "Writing and Rewriting" (**www.rachellegardner.com**), the blog of literary agent Rachelle Gardner. By offering helpful advice and interacting with her readers, she has gained national recognition for her agency and won the confidence of her potential clients.

Start your blog by registering on one of the free blog sites, such as Wordpress (**www.wordpress.com**), Blogger (**www.blogger.com**), or LiveJournal (**www.livejournal.com**). Once you have set up your account, you can select a template for your blog and begin posting. The free sites run ads alongside your blog; if you do not want ads appearing on your blog, you can pay a subscription fee. A blog has a place for you to type in your post, and then preview it before you publish it. Most blogs allow you to insert hyperlinks to websites in your posts, and many allow photos, videos, and widgets (buttons that run applications or link the viewer to another website).

Create your blog posts in Microsoft Office Word

Create your blog posts in Microsoft Office Word 2007 or 2010 and upload them directly to your blog.

- When you open a new document in Word, select "New Blog Post."

- Register a New Blog account by typing in your user name, password, and the URL of your blog.

- Use all the familiar editing features in Word to create your blog post, and insert photos (if your blog service allows photos in blogs).

- Click "Insert Category" on the menu bar at the top of the page to add categories to your post. Click the "Publish" button. Your blog post will be converted to HTML and uploaded to your blog (you must have Internet access).

Getting started is simple. As you add more and more posts, you will need to develop a system to organize your posts by categories (topics or themes). Blogs can become elaborate — some double as author websites, and you can set up a system of links to other blogs or send your latest posts out as RSS (Rich Site Summary) news feeds to subscribers. Wordpress allows users to program their own code on blogs. A professional Web designer can create a sophisticated blog template for you if you want to make blogging a central part of your marketing strategy.

No one will read your blog if they do not know it exists. As soon as you have your blog up and running, email your friends and contacts with the URL. Add your blog to your business cards, and mention it to everyone. Tweet a welcome announcement and notifications about interesting posts. Place a link to your blog on all of your social networking profiles and in the automatic signature at the bottom of your email.

Blogging Do's and Don'ts

Do:

- Post new content regularly. Blogs are dynamic by nature, so constantly refresh with new commentary, reflections, and ideas. Regular blog posts keep readers coming back and attract search-engine traffic. Three times a week (at least) is recommended.

- Start each post with a few short sentences expressing your main points, then go on to elaborate each point in a paragraph. Serialize longer posts as several smaller posts spread over a period of days. You also can link to your longer article on another page.

- Keep your posts personal and conversational as though you were communicating with friends.

- Check your blog regularly and respond to any comments. People who read your blog want to interact with you.

- Organize your blog posts by theme and topic, and use descriptive tags to help people find what they are looking for.

- Include newsworthy facts, statistics, and other factual information — this will legitimize what you say and help attract search engine traffic.

- Read and post comments on other people's blogs. You can include a link to your own blog as part of your signature. Keep a list of blogs related to your and post on them regularly.

- Make your blog lively and interesting. Add photos, videos, podcasts, or graphics when appropriate. Use guest bloggers and interviews with knowledgeable people.

- Promote your blog with email, on your business cards, on your book covers, on your Facebook page, and in your tweets.

- Create posts using short extracts from your books or material from your articles.

Don't:

- Delete a blog post once you have published it. Readers often link to your posts or recommend them to friends in email; making your post disappear will break all those links and disappoint your followers. If you realize you have spoken in error, issue a correction similar to those used by newspapers, or use strikeout to draw lines through the offending text and show the correction next to it.

- Forget to spell check a post before publishing it.

- Start a blog and then forget about it.

- Fail to respond to comments posted on your blog.

Business Cards and Email Signatures

Print business cards with your name and the title of your book, and a website address where people can learn more about you and order your book. Carry these cards with you wherever you go, include them in press kits and with cover letters, and leave them on counter displays in stores where your target audience shops.

Most email programs allow you to create an online signature that appears in every email you send out. Create an email signature with your name, the title of your book, a link to your website, and perhaps a short quote.

Write Articles for Newspapers and Magazines

Another good way to build your platform is to write articles for newspapers and magazines. Send out query letters, similar to the query letters you send to agents or publishers, to magazine and newspaper editors with your article proposals. Writer's Market (**www.writersmarket.com**) has an extensive directory of publications and their submission guidelines. If your reputation is not established enough yet to land you a regular column in a newspaper, there is still hope — sign up to write for an Internet news site such as About.com (**www.about.com**) or Examiner.com (**www.examiner.com**). You must go through an application procedure, but once you are accepted, you can develop an entire line of online articles and link them to your blogs, author pages, and book pages.

Create Author Profile Pages

Take full advantage of the author pages and profile pages on social media sites, online booksellers, and business networks. Examples include Amazon.com Author Central (**https://authorcentral.amazon.com**), your LinkedIn profile, and your Facebook profile. Upload all relevant information, including your headshot, author bio, and list of books you have published. Remember to update your profiles whenever you publish a new book. Put an article about yourself on Wikipedia (**www.wikipedia.com**) written in the third person.

Create a profile for yourself on writers' communities, such as Authors-Den.com (**www.authorsden.com**) and Harper Collins's Authonomy.com (**www.authonomy.com**).

Participate in an Author's Group

The wonderful thing about marketing books is that when readers love a genre or a topic, they want to read more. Readers are not exclusive; they do not read books by only one writer. Their bookshelves always have room for another good author. Author's groups are associations of writers who offer support to each other and collaborate to promote their books. Many are organized around a particular genre. Some author's groups organize group book tours; five or six authors doing a simultaneous book signing make a much bigger impression than one little-known author sitting at a table alone. Members share the work of organizing and publicizing the tour. A new author can piggyback on the reputation of established writers in the group by sharing their limelight.

Members of author groups actively promote each other's books on the Internet. They blog and tweet about each other, write book reviews, and place news about other authors in the group in their email newsletters. Belonging to an author group is like turbocharging your online platform. News about you and your books spreads farther, faster when you collaborate. It is also an emotional boost when fellow authors congratulate you on your accomplishments.

Author groups also increase their blog power by co-blogging. Instead of spending hours of precious time every week developing your own blog, you can schedule one good blog post on a group blog every week or two. A group blog attracts all the authors' fans and gives you more exposure than you can achieve by yourself.

Author groups also offer opportunities for mentoring, encouragement, and referrals to agents, publishers, and other services. Some author groups have an application and audition process or requirements for membership. You can find author groups online by typing keywords like "author group *your genre* blog" in a search engine. Examples of well-established author groups are Stages on Pages (**www.stagesonpages.com**) and The Elevensies (**http://2011debuts.livejournal.com**).

Monitoring Your Online Presence

As you work to build an online identity and get the word out about your writing, it helps to monitor the buzz and stay abreast of your online reputation. One thing you can do is set up Google "Alerts." Go to Google.com and select "Alerts" under "Specialized Search." (Get there by clicking "more" and then "even more" on the menu at the top of the Google screen.) Set up alerts for your name and the title of your book and for your main characters if you have them. You will receive an email notification each time those names appear on the Internet.

Set up Google alerts for topics related to your e-book. When you are alerted about a new blog post or news article on your topic, go to that URL, and enter the conversation or post a comment, using a signature that links to your author website or book page.

A variety of social media tools help you monitor your [public image in social media:

- Social Oomph (**www.TweetLater.com**): This service allows you to set up tweets in advance and schedule them to appear at a certain date and time. Free and paid options are available. Free option includes an email newsletter that lists tweets with keywords and key phrases you specify.

- Search engines for tweets: Sites such as Topsy (**http://topsy.com**) and Twazzup (**www.twazzup.com**) track your retweets and any comments about you; type in your username to search.

- Mentions: Sites like socialmention (**http://socialmention.com/alerts**) and SiteMention (**http://sitemention.com**) track social media for terms you define, and email you alerts.

- Specialized results: Addictomatic™ (**http://addictomatic.com**) provides you with a specialized results page when you type in search terms. Searches news sites, blogs, Google, YouTube, Flickr®, Digg™, Technorati, Topix, Ask®, and others.

- BoardTracker (**www.boardtracker.com**) is a search engine for forums.

- Monitoring tool: Trackur™ (**www.trackur.com**). Social media monitoring; free and paid versions.

- Reputation tracker: BrandsEye (**www.brandseye.com**), Reputation.com (**www.reputation.com/myreputationdiscovery**), and Brandwatch (**www.brandwatch.com**) track your online reputation through Twitter, online news sources, and others. Free and paid versions.

Your Author Website

It costs little to purchase a domain name and set up your own website using a template and the free design software available from companies such as GoDaddy.com® (**www.godaddy.com**), Wix.com (**www.wix.com**), Buildfree.org (**www.buildfree.org**), and Weebly.com (**www.weebly.com**). However, a professionally designed website makes a much better impression. Look at other authors' websites. When you come across a website you particularly like, make a note of the URL and look at the bottom of the home page for the designer's name and copyright information. Contact that designer and request a quote for designing your site. When you are talking to website designers, show them examples of sites you like and features you want to include on your website.

Look for a designer or website design company that has experience with author sites. An experienced Web designer already will know which software programs are most compatible and offer the best value and how to solve glitches that might keep your website from running smoothly. He or she also will know how to optimize your website so it appears near the top of search engines' result pages (SEO: search engine optimization).

Selling Books and Merchandise Online

Many e-book distributors and POD publishers will allow you to link to your own sales page on their site where customers can purchase your book. They handle all the financial transactions and pay you a royalty or a percentage of each sale.

An online shopping cart gathers and processes information for customers making purchases directly from your website. Most website design programs include a shopping cart template so you can add an online store to your site.

If you are selling merchandise, you can use shopping cart software that calculates sales tax for online sales and processes orders for as little as $30 per month.

You also will need a payment gateway, a service that takes credit card information and validates it before transferring funds to your bank account. Flagship Merchant Services® (**www.flagshipmerchant.com**), GoEmerchant (**www.goemerchant.com**), FastCharge (**www.fastcharge.com**), Merchant Warehouse (**http://merchantwarehouse.com**), Instamerchant (www.instamerchant.com) or Durango Merchant Services (**http://durangomerchantservices.com**). Consider paying extra for charge-back insurance to protect you from losses due to purchases made with stolen credit card numbers.

You can open a merchant account to receive the funds from online purchases with almost any bank. All of these services charge various service fees, transaction fees, and/or monthly subscriptions. Shop carefully, and purchase only the services you need. Make sure your shopping cart software, payment gateway, and merchant account are compatible before you make any commitments.

If you make only occasional sales, and you are not ready to set up a full-fledged e-commerce system, you can use a third-party payment system such as PayPal (**www.paypal.com**), 2Checkout (**www.2checkout.com**) or ClickBank® (**www.clickbank.com**). These companies act as payment gateway and merchant account rolled into one. Instead of monthly subscriptions or service fees, they take a commission from each transaction. These commissions are higher than the transaction fees charged by merchant accounts, but you have to pay only when you make a sale. Many third-party payment systems also process payments from customers in foreign countries.

Protect your website and your marketing efforts by registering your URL with all the appropriate endings: .net, .info, .org, and .mobi. Also register alternative spellings and possible typos; you can redirect these other domain names to your website. Many spam merchandisers and ad sites attempt to capitalize on legitimate website addresses by registering misspellings of popular URLs. Any fan who looks at your website is a potential customer; you do not want to lose even one opportunity because someone misspelled or mistyped your name. You can reserve a domain name for $6 to $10 per year, a small price to pay for protection of your name. Domain name registrations must be renewed every year. Ensure you do not lose your domain name by setting up automatic registration with your vendor.

Planning your website

Before you begin speaking with website designers, have a clear concept of how you want your website to look and function. A website designer will be guided by your vision — his or her job is to provide the technical and artistic expertise. Spend some time exploring the websites of other authors. Observe how each website is organized, where the navigation menus are located, and the ease with which you can find information. Note the way in which the author and books are presented, the color schemes, and the use of video interviews and audio excerpts. Look for features and functions you want to include in your own website.

The overall design of your website should reflect your genre and your unique qualities. Your input is important, but your personal tastes and preferences might not be the most effective for your website. For example, you might want your website to open with an impressive animation using Adobe Flash®, a multimedia platform that allows streaming of audio and video. However, visitors to your site probably want to access information as quickly as possible and may not be able to view the Flash presentation clearly on a handheld device or an older computer. A simple home page might produce better sales results and encourage visitors to view more pages on your website. An experienced website designer knows how to appeal to an audience and how to make the website easy for visitors to use (user-friendly). Listen to the suggestions of the website designer before you decide on a final design.

Your website should be created so you or someone on your staff can add new pages, edit text, update each section, maintain blogs and newsletters, change photos, and manage sales and reports without having to rely on the Web designer. Make this clear in your Web design contract, and define exactly what, if any, ongoing maintenance the Web designer will provide and the procedures for making changes to the website design. Website maintenance can take a lot of time; streamline the process by making all your websites consistent and easily accessible to the staff member who will be updating them.

Home page

Your home page is both a snapshot of your entire website and a statement about you and your book. In a few seconds, someone who opens your home page will understand what kind of book you are promoting and what information is available on your website. Your home page should be exciting and informative. The top portion of your home page, which appears in the browser screen when someone opens your website, is the most important because many readers do not stay on your website if they do not see something that interests them right away. According to Nielsen Online, the average time spent looking at a Web page is 56 seconds. You have less than a minute to grab a fan's attention.

At a glance, a visitor to your home page should see your name and the title(s) of your book(s), a captivating image of at least one book cover or an attractive headshot of you (if you are going to display your photo), and a list of the sections of your website. Do not make the images too large because that space is valuable. Most author home pages have a permanent portion that displays their name and navigation menu and an area with a blog or news articles and reviews that is changed at frequent intervals to keep fans coming back. Detailed information, biographical material, and book excerpts can be placed on other pages or in a lower section of the home page and linked to an introductory sentence or navigation bar at the top of the home page.

Navigation

Navigation refers to the way in which visitors to your website move from one page to another. Website designers know that a certain percentage of visitors leave a site each time they are required to click on a button or link to open an additional page. It is important to organize your website so your visitors quickly find what they are looking for and are able to return easily to pages they already have looked at. For example, you can place a button (a small image that can be clicked to open a new page) for buying your newest book near the top right-hand corner of your home page. Divide the functions of your website into distinct sections: an area for fans, an area for sales, an area for media and business contacts, and so on.

A navigation menu across the top or down the side of your home page links your visitors to the various sections of your website: a list of your books, your online store or sales pages, press releases for the media, reviews, contact information, and maybe a link for people who want to send you an email.

Give each area of your website a name that visitors can recognize instantly, such as "About the Author" or "Free Downloads." These names help visitors to your site find what they are looking for and also make it easier for search engines to locate your website pages.

News

A section with regularly updated news about your book and your career, such as the release date of your next book, book tour dates, and clips of newspaper articles helps engage your fans, but more important, it attracts attention from search engines such as Google and draws traffic to your website. As part of your marketing strategy, your website can be used to create anticipation for upcoming releases. This information should be located prominently on the home page and frequently updated to keep fans interested.

Store

A store displays information for items sold on the website and provides a shopping cart so customers can place orders and pay for purchases. If you write how-to books, you might increase your income by selling additional charts and posters or sell supplies through an affiliate program with a merchant who will process and ship the orders for you. Your store can link to your author pages on your POD publisher's site, or you can place these links directly on your home page.

About Us

If you are setting up as a publishing company, include an "About Us" section with information about you, the history of the company, a mission statement, and anything else that you want to communicate officially to the public. This is a good place to put your résumé and qualifications. This section also might include links to your contact information or media press kits.

Community

Some authors encourage readers to become involved in an online community by posting comments in a blog or message board and signing up for social media. A community section also can contain information about book tours, your latest projects, or general news items about the publishing industry. When visitors to your website are allowed to contribute to an online community and interact with other readers, they develop a stronger loyalty to you and your books. Maintaining a community requires a regular investment of time, but it can help build your Internet presence and establish your reputation as an authority in your genre. This area can connect fans to you on Twitter or Facebook.

Email newsletters

Email is a powerful way to communicate with loyal readers. Encourage them to add their email addresses to your address list, and send out newsletters informing them about your book tours, media appearances, and upcoming releases. Email recipients often forward interesting newsletters to their friends and family. You also can use your email list to learn about your fans by documenting their responses to special offers and their use of coupons.

Media and press kits

Create a section specifically for the news media where you can post press releases, announcements, and official photos for use in newspapers, magazines, and newsletters. If you do not want to make this material available to the public, put a request form on this page so journalists can contact you and get a special login to download photos and documents. When you send out email notifications or press releases, you can refer journalists to this area of your site to get photos and additional information. This will save you from having to respond to dozens of individual requests.

Favorite links

Your website can include an area where you put links to your favorite websites, blogs, and articles. Putting links to useful resources and articles on your site shows you want to help your readers with their own research and can increase your reputation as an authority in your field. A list like this can help you build a community around your website, and it allows you to exchange links with other authors and websites, who reciprocate by putting a link to your site on their websites. Traffic to and from your site to other websites is one of the factors search engines use to rank the popularity of your site. Remember, though, that when a visitor clicks on one of those links, he or she is going to someone else's website and leaving yours.

Extras

Depending on your genre and the type of books you write, you can offer bonus material for your readers, such as book excerpts, text cut out of the original manuscript before publication, additional stories about your characters, maps and pictures, or free mini e-books written just for this purpose. If your book is nonfiction, you can include links to useful websites, updates, downloadable graphics such as plans and patterns, templates for contracts and forms, and other material that ties in with your book but was too cumbersome to be included in it. Make the extras fun and be creative — you could create playlists of music to go along with your book that readers can listen to on Pandora® (**www.pandora.com**) or Playlist.com (**www. playlist.com**); recipes that match the theme of your book; drawings of the clothing and fashions worn by characters in a book; historical backgrounds; or scrapbooks or journals "created" by your characters.

Videos and book trailers

Just as a movie trailer gives audiences a taste of what they will experience when they watch a movie, a book trailer gives readers a taste of your book. A book trailer is a video promoting your book. It can be a video of you (or someone else) reading your book copy or excerpts from your book, a short movie related to your book, or a slide show. You do not need an elaborate book trailer; a well-made home video can be effective. You can have more than one book trailer for the same book.

Contact Us

This is an important page. It establishes how the public can communicate with you. If you do not want to receive phone calls, you can supply visitors with a form for submitting email inquiries. You or someone on your staff should check inquiries every day — you do not want to miss an opportunity for publicity.

Advertising

Although most author websites do not carry advertising, you could make extra income by selling advertising space on your site for products and services relevant to your book topic. You also can advertise your own books or merchandise in a space along the side of each page.

Business and distribution

Depending on your distribution channels, you might need an area on your site where distributors or individual retailers can place orders, make payments, and print out invoices and statements. If you are selling hard copies of your book through a POD publisher, you can set up discount codes for wholesale orders and put links from your website to the POD publisher's order forms.

Website analytics

Once your website goes live, monitor it regularly to see how many fans are coming to your site and which areas attract the most attention. The analysis of website traffic is a science in itself. You probably do not need to go into depth, but a few simple observations can be useful. Page views refers to the number of times someone opens a page on a website. Click-through paths show how visitors to your site move from your home page to the other areas of the site. A click-through rate is the percentage of visitors who click a link on one page to open and view another page. If one page or area of your site is receiving a large number of page views, it might indicate that your readers are especially interested in that topic. It also could mean you are receiving attention in a news article or another website that is directing readers to that page on your website. You may be able to capitalize on this interest by making this part of your website more prominent.

Low click-through rates from your home page to other areas of your site could indicate that visitors are losing interest after they see your home page and that you need to try a different "look" or approach. Low click-through rates also could indicate technical problems, such as a graphic that takes too long to load in a browser. Test this by trying to open the page in other browsers and on other computers with different operating systems and software. When visitors start to buy your book and then fail to complete their orders, they might be having difficulty with their credit card payments or difficulty filling out the order form.

Most website design software includes some reporting and traffic analysis features. Google Analytics (**www.google.com/support/analytics**) allows you to track conversion data, analyze the flow of visitors through your site, and identify elements of your site that could be changed to improve visitor retention, and is free for websites with fewer than five million page views per month. If you decide you need a detailed, in-depth analysis of traffic through your website, you can purchase a website analysis software program or service from a company such as Webtrends® (**www.webtrends. com**), Alexa (**www.alexa.com**), or Adobe Web analytics powered by Omniture (**www.omniture.com/en/products/online_analytics**).

Search Engine Optimization (SEO)

Whenever you are writing for your website, be conscious of the search engines your readers will use to find it. Keep the text on your home page and main topic pages simple, and include all the keywords people might type into a search engine: your name, your book titles, the topic(s) covered in your book, your genre, the names of important characters or series, and any other terms commonly associated with your books. Save your creative writing, esoteric verbiage, and personal reflections for the interior pages of your site. Avoid empty content such as "Welcome to my website!" or "This is the place where you will find…."

Links to and from other websites help establish your rank on search engines as a popular website. Place links to your website on all your profiles, social media pages, blogs, and email signatures. Make sure your website is associated with your name when it appears in the media. One of the most effective ways to boost traffic to your website is to be featured in a well-known newspaper or online news source. Although it is difficult to get a book review in a newspaper, you can attract publicity by submitting an interesting story suggestion or press release about your career or your book topic.

Your website is a central focus of your online marketing strategy, but it is only one component. It will not make your book successful all by itself. A website is a tool to be used, together with social media, aggressive media promotion, and live appearances, to gain the attention of your readers and the publishing industry. Schedule regular website maintenance on your calendar so your website remains up-to-date and attracts visitors with fresh information that corresponds to your most recent press releases.

What's Next?

This book has familiarized you with the process of writing and publishing an e-book.

In the last four years, e-books have brought about such dramatic changes in the publishing world that it is difficult to imagine what the future holds. But one thing is for sure: E-books are here to stay. They will take over an increasing share of the market for books and change the way books are marketed, sold, and read, but they will never completely replace print. Writers who stay informed of the latest trends and developments in the publishing industry will be able to discover new opportunities and keep themselves ahead of the crowd.

E-book publishing has become a great equalizer for writers, just as MP3 files leveled the playing field for musicians a few years ago. No longer do authors have to spend time and money submitting manuscripts to agents and editors, hoping to find someone who will see their books as a viable business prospect, and then wait another year or two to see their books come on the market. Now a book can be marketed directly to the public, and readers decide which books have merit. A self-published author, however, does not have a staff of experienced professionals working to launch a highly marketable product on a national scale. Instead, the author is responsible for every aspect of producing and marketing the book, and the author's lack of expertise may result in failure even when the book itself is worthy.

Another lesson can be taken from the history of do-it-yourself music recordings on the Internet. Within a year, millions of homemade recordings were competing for attention on the Internet. In order to maintain a quality listening experience for its customers, iTunes had to implement a system to screen out amateurs. Anyone can self-publish an e-book, no matter how badly written and full of errors it might be. Today, e-book retail sites rely on reader reviews and sampling to direct customers to readable, well-edited books. The time may come soon when major book retailers like Amazon and Barnes & Noble will start enforcing editorial standards and excluding novice writers.

Authors and traditional publishers alike worry that illegal file sharing will seriously erode their income from e-books, as it has eroded sales of music recordings in the music industry. It is too soon to tell how closely the publishing industry will follow the music industry. Indie authors favor getting their books into the hands of as many readers as possible over making sure every reader pays in the belief that a widespread reputation generates book sales. Traditional publishers enforce DRM because they must recoup the expenses of bringing a book to market. Because printed words are not consumed in the same way as music, the e-book industry might develop entirely new income streams for authors and publishers.

The Internet does not have physical boundaries. E-books can be accessed from almost any location where e-reading technology exists. Though copyright laws and payment systems differ from country to country, the time will come when many of these barriers are transcended, making it possible for writers to reach audiences in many parts of the world simultaneously.

The ability to search digital files ensures the future of e-books. In a few seconds, Internet search engines can scan the entire content of every e-book and locate the exact information a reader wants. Never before have readers had so much information at their fingertips. Quotes from ancient texts, data from the latest scientific studies, obscure historical facts — nothing is out of reach if it is in print somewhere.

Whether you publish your e-book yourself or employ someone to do it for you, become involved. Learn as much as you can about every aspect of the publishing business. The more you know about writing, book design, formatting, promotion, social media, and the Internet, the better you will be prepared for every new opportunity when it arises. Take your place today as one of the international community of authors who keep us entertained, informed, inspired, and excited about life.

Genre Definitions

Fiction

action thriller: A story that incorporates a ticking-clock scenario and violent battle scenes.

alternate history: A novel that speculates on historical events.

amateur detective: A mystery story solved by someone who is not a detective.

Arthurian fantasy: A story that features the legend of King Arthur and the Knights of the Round Table.

autobiography: An account of a person's life written by the subject.

Bangsian fantasy: A novel that speculates on the afterlives of famous people.

biopunk: A story that blends noir, Japanese anime, and post-modern elements to create an underground, nihilistic biotech society.

chick-lit: Humorous romantic adventures designed for female readers in their 20s and 30s.

child in peril: Mystery or horror stories that involve the abduction or abuse of a child.

children's fantasy: A fantasy story written specifically for young readers.

Christian romance: Romances in which both the hero and heroine are Christians who adhere to Christian ideals.

classic whodunit: A story in which a detective solves the crime, with the author presenting numerous clues for the reader.

comic horror: Novels that spoof horror conventions or present the horror with elements of dark humor.

comic mystery/bumbling detective: A mystery story featuring humor in which the detective is incompetent but somehow manages to solve the crime anyway.

comic sci-fi/fantasy: A story the either spoofs the fantasy or science fiction genre or incorporates humorous elements.

comic thriller: Either includes comedic elements or spoofs the thriller/suspense genre.

commercial fiction: Novels that appeal to a wide audience.

conspiracy: A thriller in which the hero or heroine uncovers a conspiracy by a large, powerful group.

contemporary romance: A romance with modern characters and true-to-life settings.

courtroom drama: A mystery tale that centers on the justice system; usually the hero is a defense attorney who must prove his client's innocence.

cozy: A mystery tale that takes place in a small town or home where all the suspects are present and familiar with one another, except the detective, who is usually an outsider.

creepy kids: A horror story in which children are controlled by dark forces and turn against adults.

crime thriller: A tale that focuses on the commission of a crime, often from the point of view of the perpetrators.

cyberpunk: Sci-fi stories that feature tough outsiders in a high-tech, dehumanized future setting.

dark fantasy: Fantasy tales that focus on the darker side of magic, incorporating violence and elements of horror or a horror story that incorporates supernatural and fantasy elements.

dark mystery/noir: Hardboiled detective stories presented in an urban setting with morally ambiguous characters.

disaster: A story that presents natural elements as the antagonist, such as an earthquake or hurricane.

dystopian: Fantasy or sci-fi stories that present a bleak future world.

eco-thriller: A story in which the hero must battle an ecological catastrophe and the people who created it.

erotica or **romantica:** A romance story that depicts explicit sexual scenes.

erotic fantasy: Fantasy tales that focus on sexuality.

erotic thriller: A suspense in which sexual aspects are a major part of the story.

erotic vampire: Emphasizes the sexuality in a vampire story and includes graphic violence.

espionage: A thriller/suspense in which the hero is an international spy.

espionage mystery: A story that incorporates elements of the international spy novel but focuses more on the puzzle that must be solved.

fabulist: A horror tale where objects, animals, or forces are given human characteristics to deliver a moral message.

fantasy: Fiction that features elements of magic, wizardry, and the supernatural.

forensic: A thriller or mystery story that features forensic experts and focuses on forensic labs and detailed scientific procedures.

game-related fantasy: Stories based on a specific role-playing game, such as Dungeons and Dragons.

glitz/glamour: A romance story that follows elite celebrity-like characters as they live a glamorous life traveling around the world.

gothic: A story that combines elements of horror and romance with medieval props, such as castles, darkness, and decay.

hard science fiction: Tales set in the future that incorporate real-life, current-day science.

hauntings: A horror tale that focuses on a structure possessed by a ghost, demon, or poltergeist.

heists and capers: A crime tale that focuses on the planning and execution of a crime, told from the criminal's perspective.

heroic fantasy: A tale that focuses on the heroes of fantastical wars.

high/epic fantasy: Stories that feature a young hero battling an evil entity to save the fate of an entire race or nation.

historical: A novel that takes place in a true-to-life period of history, with emphases on the details of the setting. Sub-genres may include historical thriller, historical horror, and historical romance.

horror: A story that evokes fear and/or revulsion using supernatural or psychological elements.

horror thriller: A thriller/suspense in which the antagonist is a monster-villain and includes graphic violence.

how-to: A book that offers the reader specific instructions, information, and advice to accomplish a goal.

inverted: A mystery story in which the reader knows who committed the crime.

legal thriller: A tale in which the hero is a lawyer that uses his skills to battle the bad guys.

locked room: A mystery tale in which the crime is apparently committed under impossible circumstances.

magical realism: A horror story where dark forces or creatures exist in real-life settings.

medical mystery: A story that involves a medical threat or illegal use of medical technology.

medical thriller: Either a tale in which the hero is in the medical profession and uses his skills to battle the antagonist or a story that features the illegal or immoral use of medical technology.

memoir: An author's commentary on the people and events that influenced a specific phase of his life.

military science fiction: Tales of war set in the future that incorporate real-life, current-day military technology.

military thriller: A story in which the hero is a member of the military working as part of a specialized force.

multicultural romance: A romance centered on non-Caucasian characters, most often African-American or Hispanic.

mundane science fiction: Tales that include only scientific knowledge that is known to actually exist.

mystery science fiction: Either a science-fiction tale with a central

mystery or a classic mystery story with science fiction elements.

mystery thriller: A suspense mystery with an international story and lots of action.

mythic fiction: Fantasy stories inspired by classic myths, legends, or fairy tales.

new age (fiction): A fantasy novel that speculates on occult subjects, such as astrology, psychic phenomena, spiritual healing, UFOs, and mysticism.

paranormal: Includes supernatural elements, such as time travel or characters with psychic abilities.

police procedural: A crime thriller or mystery story that focuses on the processes of real-life police procedures and is told from the perspective of the police as they work a case.

political intrigue: A thriller in which the hero must ensure the safety of the government.

post-apocalyptic: Science fiction tales that focus on the struggle to survive on earth after an apocalypse.

private detective: A mystery in which the crime is solved by a private investigator.

psychological horror: A tale based on an insane or psychologically disturbed character that is often a human-monster.

psychological suspense: A mystery that focuses on the details of the crime and what motivated the perpetrator to commit the crime.

psychological thriller: A suspense that highlights the emotional and mental conflict between the hero and the villain.

quiet horror: A story that uses atmosphere and mood to elicit fear and create suspense, rather than graphic description.

religious horror: A story that incorporates religious icons and mythology, such as angels and demons.

religious sci-fi/fantasy: A science fiction or fantasy novel that centers on theological ideas and heroes who are ruled by religious beliefs.

romance: Novels that feature love stories.

romance sci-fi: A science fiction story in which romance is central to the plot.

romantic comedy: A romance focused on humor.

romantic mystery: A mystery tale in which the crime-solvers are romantically involved.

romantic suspense: A romance tale that includes a heroine who may have to solve a crime or mystery.

romantic thriller: A suspense novel in which the protagonists are romantically involved.

science fantasy: A fantasy story in which the fantastical elements are supported by scientific explanations.

science fiction: Novels that incorporate elements of science or pseudo-science.

science fiction/fantasy: A designation used by booksellers to collapse two separate genres into one for marketing purposes.

science-fiction horror: A tale that deals with alien invasions, mad scientists, or out-of-control experiments.

sensual: A romance story based on the sensual tension between the hero and heroine.

social science fiction: Stories that focus on how characters react to their environments.

soft science fiction: Stories based on softer sciences such as psychology, sociology, and anthropology.

space opera: A science fiction tale with traditional heroes and villains and plenty of action scenes.

spicy: A romance that involves a married couple.

splatter/splatterpunk: A horror novel that presents extremely explicit scenes and gruesome violence.

spy-fi: Espionage stories with science fiction elements, such as high-tech gadgets.

steampunk: A sci-fi/fantasy tale that presents an alternate history in which characters in Victorian England have access to 20th century technology.

superheroes: Fantasy or science fiction tale featuring characters with superhuman abilities.

supernatural menace: A horror story featuring supernatural elements, such as ghosts, demons, vampires, and werewolves, which cause mayhem.

supernatural thriller: A suspense in which the hero or the antagonist (or both) have supernatural powers.

suspense: Novels that use elements of suspense to solve a crime or unravel a mystery.

sweet: A romance with a heroine who is a virgin.

sword and sorcery: A classic fantasy tale set in medieval period that incorporates wizardry.

technological thriller: A suspense in which out-of-control technology is central to the plot.

technology horror: A horror tale that features technology out of control.

technothriller: A thriller mystery that emphasizes high technology.

thriller: A novel that uses suspense to tell the story and incorporates a plot structure that focuses gamesmanship and centers on hunt-and-chase scenes.

thriller science fiction: A sci-fi novel that incorporates elements of a classic thriller story.

time-travel: Science fiction tales based on the concept of moving backward or forward through time and into parallel worlds.

urban fantasy: A story in which characters with magical powers appear in a normal modern setting (similar to magical realism).

vampire fantasy: A fantasy novel that incorporates the classic vampire story, focusing on sexuality and romantic liaisons, without the horror elements.

weird tales: A horror tale that features strange and uncanny events.

western: a story set in the North American, South American, or Australian West.

woman in jeopardy: A mystery story in which the heroine is placed in peril by a crime and struggles to triumph over the perpetrator.

wuxia: Fantasy stories that incorporate martial arts and Chinese philosophies.

young adult: Books written specifically for teenagers, ages 12 to 17, with heroes the same age as the readers.

young adult horror: Horror stories written specifically for teenagers. They include heroes that are young adults and are less violent than traditional horror tales.

young adult mystery: Mystery stories written specifically for teenagers. They include a young adult hero detective who pursues criminals that are usually less violent than those in adult mystery novels.

young adult romance: A romance written specifically for teenagers. They include a hero and heroine who are young adults and contain little sexual content.

zombie: Horror tales featuring dead people who come "alive" and torment the living.

Non-Fiction

adventure: Adventure books consist of a man-against-nature story. They have an extreme and dramatic quality and are set in an exotic location.

biography: A carefully researched account of someone's life, or a period in someone's life. Biographies require the author to be devoted to the subject matter but objective enough to go wherever the truth may lead in order to create an accurate portrayal.

coffee table: Large-sized print books intended for display on a coffee table that contain more photographs and illustrations than text. This concept is difficult to reproduce as an e-book because of its emphasis on graphics. Common sub-genres are architecture, art, and photography.

cooking and food: To succeed in this competitive genre, you need a distinctive theme that captures the reader's attention. Cookbooks incorporate vibrant photos, systematic detailed instructions, and a casual "you-can-do-it" style.

history: History books have a scholarly tone and often are written by experts.

how-to: A book filled with instructions, valuable information, tips, suggestions, examples, and illustrations. Information is presented sequentially with each chapter supporting the overall concept. These books conclude with the reader achieving the "goal."

humor: Humor books are filled with content that is witty and entertaining. They are short, funny, and have an identifiable audience.

inspirational/religious/spiritual/metaphysical: Religious, inspirational, and spiritual books share themes of a particular belief system and provide wisdom, motivation, and advice to guide readers to live a full life in harmony with specific concepts.

medical and science: Medical and science books enlighten and educate readers about the medical and scientific fields. They incorporate charts, graphs, illustrations, and a thorough glossary.

memoir: A personal account, tragic or inspiring, that transcends the personal and becomes a shared experience for readers.

military: A sub-genre of history, covering in detail some aspect of military history, science, or experience.

narrative nonfiction: Truthful writing that reads like a novel, containing factual subject matter and characterized by exhaustive research and a compelling narrative or a literary prose style.

reference: Reference books contain authoritative facts and are updated regularly.

self-help: Self-help books encompass the realm of psychology and contain more practical examples than how-to books. The most popular category is relationships. The author's style is casual, as if conversing with an old friend across the table.

travel guide: Travel guides require detailed research and must provide all the necessary information and tips to help the reader successfully plan a trip to the destination. They can be formal guides or contain casual, conversational advice.

travelogue: A book describing the author's personal travel experience. Travelogues may include travel guide details about the destination.

Glossary

ABI: Advance Book Information. A service providing a directory and database listing for your book that can be accessed by booksellers, librarians, and distributors.

ancillary materials: Additional or supplemental materials, often packaged with educational books and textbooks. Can include maps, charts, and other teaching aids.

app: A computer program that presents a book as an interactive software application rather than a document.

ASIN (Amazon Standard Identification Number): A number assigned by Amazon to every product sold through its website.

back matter: Material that appears in the back of a book. Includes production notes, author biography, and other matter to be included at the publisher's discretion.

beta reader: A person who reads your manuscript and gives you feedback while you are still working on it.

bricks-and-mortar: A retailer that has a physical premises, such as Barnes & Noble, as opposed to a retailer that sells only online.

byte: The amount of electronic storage space occupied by a single typed character.

chunking: The practice of breaking information down and presenting it as individual concepts and ideas.

CIP: Cataloging in Publication Record. It is a record the Library of Congress prepares in order for libraries and book dealers to process, catalog, organize, and place a printed book.

color theory: The relation, mixing, and harmony of colors, often with consideration to where they are placed on a color wheel.

copy editor: An editor who corrects grammatical mistakes, typographical errors and improper word usage, checks the accuracy of facts, and notes inconsistencies in style and syntax.

copyright: The legal right to ownership of original created material.

critique partner: A fellow writer who comments on your work in exchange for your feedback on his or her writing.

CSS (Cascading Style Sheet): The standards that define the appearance of Web pages in an Internet browser.

desktop publishing: A term used to describe publishing tasks that can be handled by PC computer software and a printer.

developmental editor: An editor who makes recommendations about the content and organization of a book, rewrites passages to improve clarity, and helps the author develop an initial concept or idea.

division: A group of imprints that form a department of a publishing house.

dots per inch (DPI): A measure of the resolution of print images, based on the number of ink dots per square inch.

DRM (digital rights management): Software technology that allows e-book retailers to control how and where an e-book can be read.

drop cap: The use of a large decorative capital letter for the first sentence in each chapter.

editor: The person who oversees the production of a book, advises the author about content, grammar, and writing style, and proofreads and makes corrections.

folio: A series of pages created by folding a large printed sheet of paper in half.

front matter: The material in the beginning of the book that precedes the story, including the copyright notice, dedication, and title page.

gross sales: Sales calculated based on the retail price of the book.

gutter: The inner margins of a bound book; the white space created by two facing pages in the center of the book near the binding.

hand selling: Selling books directly to customers at an event or a book fair.

honorarium: A fee paid to a visiting author for speaking or presenting.

hybrid: A book that belongs to two or more genres.

imagesetting: The process of setting up a page for printing as a high-resolution digital image.

imprint: A specialized subdivision of a publishing house that focuses on a certain area and often carries a certain identity.

ISBN (International Standard Book Number): A unique ID number assigned to each new book and used to catalog books and track book sales.

kilobyte: About 1,024 bytes.

layout: An arrangement of the graphic elements of a printed book.

LCCN (Library of Congress Control Number): These are used for authority, bibliographic, and classification records and are currently structured according to length, elements, and position.

leading: The space between printed lines.

licensing agreement: Allows a publisher to sell an idea to other companies, sometimes resulting in character and story offshoots.

line: Part of an imprint at a publishing house that sometimes includes series of books.

line editor: An editor who reads each line of text and corrects grammatical mistakes, typographical errors, and incorrect word usage.

list price: Price on the cover of the book and in retail catalogs.

manuscript: A writer's original work.

markup language: Annotations inserted in a text file that describe how the text will be presented to the viewer.

megabyte (MB): Approximately one million bytes.

megapublisher: A large publishing conglomerate owned by a media syndicate.

NCX (Navigation Control file for XML): A file that provides an external navigational menu for an e- book.

noncompete clause: A clause in a publishing contract that prevents the author from publishing a similar book without the publisher's permission.

novelette: A fiction book of 7,500 to 40,000 words, with a plot more complex than that of a short story, usually written without chapters.

novelty books: Books with added features beyond traditional binding, commonly issued from toy companies and mass-market publishers.

net sales: Sales calculated based on the net profit made from each sale (retail price minus production costs).

offset printing: A method of printing in which plates are used for ink printing.

oral tradition: The passing down of stories and tales by spoken word.

paperback: A book with a paper cover.

PCN: Preassigned control number

PDF (Portable Document Format): A file format that captures all the elements of a print book in an electronic file.

pixel: The smallest unit of a digital or screen display.

pixels per inch (PPI): A measure of the resolution of a digital or screen display.

postpublication review: Intended for the consumer; appears after the book's release to the public.

prepublication review: A review that releases before the book.

pre-writing: Anything you do to help the writing along, such as character outlines, brainstorming, and note taking.

print-on-demand (POD): A printing process in which books are printed as customers order them.

print quantity needed (PQN): A digital printing process that uses laser printing and toner to produce small quantities of commercial-quality books.

pulp fiction magazines: Magazines popular during the first half of the 20th century that were printed on cheap pulp paper and contained novels and short stories.

recto: The right page of a manuscript.

reflowable: The ability of text to automatically wrap to the next line to adapt to the window size and margins of an e-reader.

remaindering: Selling copies of a print book at a discount before it goes out of print.

SAN: Standard Address Number.

surge title: A book that experiences a temporary surge of popularity, such as celebrity biography or an event tie-in.

tie-in: A book that carries the theme of another form of media, such as a movie, TV show, comic book, video game or public event.

TOC: Table of contents.

unit break: The number of books that must sell before an author receives a higher royalty rate.

unsolicited/unagented: Work that is without publisher solicitation or agent representation.

verso: The left page of a manuscript.

watermarking: A technique for inserting information about the buyer or the source of an e-book among the e-book files so that it can be retrieved later.

widget: A small software application that can be installed and run within a website.

word lists: Lists of curriculum-centered words teachers are required to include in classroom reading and instructional materials.

WPI: Work in progress

XML (Extensible Markup Language): A set of rules for encoding a text document in a form readable by a machine.

Further Reading

Associations

American Christian Fiction Writers (**www.acfw.com**)

American Christian Writers (**www.acwriters.com**)

American Crime Writers League (**www.acwl.org**)

Association of American Publishers (**www.publishers.org**)

Association of American University Presses (**www.aaupnet.org**)

Association of Author Representatives (AAR) (**http://aaronline.org**)

Chick Lit Writers (**www.chicklitwriters.com**)

Graphic Artists Guild (**www.graphicartistsguild.org**)

Historical Novel Society (**www.historicalnovelsociety.org**)

Horror Writers Association (**www.horror.org**)

International Association of Crime Writers (**www.crimewritersna.org**)

International Autobiography/ Biography Association (**www.iaba.org.cn**)

International Digital Publishing Forum (IDPF) (**http://idpf.org**)

International Food, Wine, and Travel Writers Association (**www.ifwtwa.org**)

International Thriller Writers Association (**www.thrillerwriters.org**)

Mystery Writers of America (**www.mysterywriters.org**)

National Association of Memoir Writers (**www.namw.org**)

National Association of Women Writers (**www.naww.org**)

National Writers Association (**www.nationalwriters.com**)

PEN (**www.pen.org**)

Poets & Writers, Inc. (**www.pw.org**)

Publishers Marketing Association (**www.pma-online.org**)

Romance Writers of America (**www.rwa.org**)

Science Fiction and Fantasy Writers of America (**www.sfwa.org**)

Sisters in Crime (**www.sistersincrime.org**)

Small Publishers Association of North America (SPAN) (**www.spannet.org**)

Society of Children's Book Writers and Illustrators (**www.scbwi.org**)

Society of Photographers and Artists Representatives (**www.spar.org**)

The Authors Guild (**www.authorsguild.or**g)

The Children's Book Council (**www.cbcbooks.org**)

The National Writers Union (**www.nwu.org**)

The Society of Children's Book Writers and Illustrators (SCBWI) (**www.scbwi.org**)

Western Writers of America, Inc. (**www.westernwriters.org**)

Writers Guild of America, West (WGAW) labor union for screen and entertainment writers (**www.wga.org**)

Bibliography

EasyBib (**www.easybib.com**)

WorldCat (**www.worldcat.org**)

Big Six Publishers

Hachette Book Group (HBG)
(**www.hachettebookgroup.com**)

HarperCollins Publishers
(**www.harpercollins.com**)

Macmillan
(**http://us.macmillan.com**)

Penguin
(**http://us.penguingroup.com**)

Random House, Inc.
(**www.randomhouse.com**)

Simon & Schuster
(**www.simonandschuster.com**)

Blog Sites and Author Groups

AuthorsDen.com
(**www.authorsden.com**)

Blogger (**www.blogger.com**)

BookGlutton
(**www.bookglutton.com**)

Google Blog Search
(**www.google.com/blogsearch**)

Harper Collins's Authonomy.com
(**www.authonomy.com**)

LiveJournal
(**www.livejournal.com**)

Self Publishing Review
(**www.selfpublishingreview.com**)

Stages on Pages
(**www.stagesonpages.com**)

Technorati
(**http://technorati.com**)

The Elevensies (**http://2011
debuts.livejournal.com**)

Wordpress (**www.wordpress.com**)

Blog tracking

Addictomatic
(**http://addictomatic.com**)

Alterian SM2
(**http://sm2.techrigy.com/main**)

Blog pulse (**http://blogpulse.com**)

BoardTracker
(**www.boardtracker.com**)

BrandsEye (**www.brandseye.com**)

Brandwatch
(**www.brandwatch.com**)

Reputation.com (**www.reputation.
com/myreputationdiscovery**)

SiteMention (**http://sitemention.com**)

Social Oomph (**www.TweetLater.com**)

socialmention (**http://socialmention.com/alerts**)

Topsy (**http://topsy.com**)

Trackur (**www.trackur.com**)

Twazzup (**www.twazzup.com**)

Book Design

EasyBib bibliography (**www.easybib.com**)

Identifont — Online digital font directory (**www.identifont.com**)

InDesign Magazine

Lyon, Jack M. *Typesetting in Microsoft Word.* (**www.selfpublishing.com/ design/downloads/articles/ typesetting.pdf**)

Microsoft Office 2007 PDF add-in (**www.microsoft.com/download/ en/details.aspx?id=7**)

Microsoft templates (**http://office. microsoft.com/en-us/templates/ default.aspx**)

Microtype printable typographic ruler (**http://www.microtype. com/typometer.html**)

PDF Desk (**www.pdfdesk.com/ winpdf.html**)

PrimoPDF® (**www.primopdf.com/ index.aspx**)

Self-Publishing Information and Resources by Jera Publishing LLC (**www.self-pub.net/templates. html**)

Worldcat bibliography (**www.worldcat.org**)

Book Scanning

BlueLeaf Book Scanning (**www. blueleaf-book-scanning.com**)

Bound Book Scanning (**http:// boundbookscanning.com**)

CSP Book Scanning Services (**http://www.cspdocscan.com**)

Bookkeeping

IRS Publication 583: Starting a Business and Keeping Records. IRS. gov. (**www.irs.gov/pub/irs-pdf/p583.pdf**)

Microsoft Excel templates (**http://office.microsoft.com/en-us/templates#**)

SBA local branches (**www.sba.gov/content/find-local-sba-office**)

Small Business Administration free online classes (**www.sba.gov/content/recordkeeping**)

Business and Taxes

"Do You Have to Pay Sales Tax on Internet Purchases?" Findlaw. com. (**http://smallbusiness.findlaw.com/business-operations/internet/internet-taxes.html**)

If You Are Self-Employed. SSA Publication No. 05-10022. January 2011. ICN 454900. **www.ssa.gov/pubs/10022.html**.

IRS Publication 547: Casualties, Disasters and Thefts (**www.irs.gov/pub/irs-pdf/p547.pdf**)

IRS Schedule SE (Form 1040): Self-Employment Tax. (**www.irs.gov/pub/irs-pdf/f1040sse.pdf**)

Register Your Fictitious or "Doing Business As" (DBA) Name, (**www.sba.gov/content/register-your-fictitious-or-doing-business-dba-name**)

SBA.gov's *Business Licenses and Permits Search Tool* (**www.sba.gov/content/search-business-licenses-and-permits**)

Topic 554 — Self-Employment Tax. (**www.irs.gov/taxtopics/tc554.html**)

Copyright and Public Domain

Creative Commons (**http://creativecommons.org**)

License Music Now.com (**http://licensemusicnow.com**)

"Understanding Copyright and Related Rights," World Intellectual Property Organization (WIPO) (**www.wipo.int/freepublications/en/intproperty/909/wipo_pub_909.html**)

eCO Tips (**www.copyright.gov/eco/tips.pdf**)

U.S. Copyright Office (**www.copyright.gov**)

Cover Design

Cover Factory (**www.coverfactory.com**)

EBook Template Source (**www.ebooktemplatesource.com/free-ebook-covers.html**)

My eCover Maker (**www.myecovermaker.com**) (subscription-based templates)

Data Storage

Microsoft (**http://office.microsoft.com/en-us/excel-help**)

Mozy® (**www.mozy.com**)

SugarSync (**www.sugarsync.com**)

Directories

American Bookseller's Association (ABA) Book Buyer's Handbook (**www.bookweb.org/handbook**) For publishers with at least three books in print.

Book Dealers Dropship Directory (**www.bookmarketingprofits.com/DSDirectory.html**) Used by online and mail-order booksellers

Books in Print (**www.bowker.com**) You will be listed automatically in Books in Print when you obtain an ISBN number from Bowker.

Book Trade in Canada and *Canadian Publishers Directory* (**www.quillandquire.com**)

International Directory of Little Magazines and Small Presses (**www.dustbooks.com/d.htm**) For self-publishers and small press listings

Small Press Record of Books in Print (**www.dustbooks.com/sr.htm**)

E-Book Design

Cover Factory (**www.coverfactory.com**)

eBook Crossroads.com (**www.ebookcrossroads.com/epublishers.html**)

EBook Template Source (**www.ebooktemplatesource.com/free-ebook-covers.html**)

EPIC
(**http://ebooks.epicauthors.com**)

My eCover Maker
(**www.myecovermaker.com**)
(subscription-based templates)

ScribD (**www.scribd.com**)

Smashwords
(**www.smashwords.com**)

E-book Retail Stores

Amazon.com (**www.amazon.com**)

Barnes & Noble
(**www.barnesandnoble.com**)

BooksOnBoard
(**www.booksonboard.com**)

Ebooks.com (**www.ebooks.com**)

Google eBooks (**http://books.
google.com/ebooks**)

Kobo (**www.kobobooks.com**)

ReaderStore — SONY
(**http://ebookstore.sony.com**)

Smashwords
(**www.smashwords.com**)

Editing

Brown, Renni and David King.
Self-Editing for Fiction Writers

Elizabeth Lyons. *Manuscript
Makeover: Revision Techniques No
Fiction Writer Can Afford To Ignore*

William Strunk Jr. *The Elements
of Style.* (**www.bartleby.com/141/
index.html**)

EPUB

2epub.com (**www.2epub.com**)

Epubcheck (**http://code.google.
com/p/epubcheck**)

IDPF (International Digital
Publishing Forum) (**www. http://
idpf.org**)

Smashwords
(**www.smashwords.com**)

Word2EPUB (**www.web-books.
com/Publishing/Word2EPUB.
htm**)

Formatting
and HTML

Taco (**http://tacosw.com**)

YemuZip (**www.yellowmug.com/ yemuzip**) A user-friendly zip option for Microsoft Windows™

Forums and Communities

Absolute Write (**http://absolutewrite.com**)

For Writers (**www.forwriters.com**)

Good Reads (**www.goodreads.com**)

Library Thing (**www.librarything.com**)

Writers Beat (**www.writersbeat.com**)

Freelancers

Elance.com (**www.elance.com**)

Guru.com (**www.guru.com**)

Hireanillustrator.com (**www.hireanillustrator.com**)

Monster.com® (**www.monster.com**)

HTML and CSS

HTML 4.01 Quick List — W3schools.com (**www.w3schools. com/html/html_quick.asp**)

WC3 HTML Markup Validation Service (free) (**http://validator.w3.org**)

CSS Reference — W3schools.com (**www.w3schools.com/cssref**)

Images and Graphics

Creative Commons (to locate images on Creative Commons, visit **http://search.creativecommons. org**)

Getty Images (**www.gettyimages. com/CreativeImages/RoyaltyFree**)

Illustration Works (**www.illustrationworks.com**)

iStockphoto (**www.istockphoto.com**)

Jupiter Images (**www.jupiterimages.com**)

Katzman Stock (**http://katzmanstock.com**)

Mira (**http://library.mira.com**)

Photos.com (**www.photos.com**)

Picasa (**http://picasa.google.com**)

Thinkstock
(**www.thinkstockphotos.com**)

Time Tunnel
(**www.timetunnel.com**)

Insurance

"Online Publishing Risks Create
Need for Libel Insurance." Michael
Rothberg. 2004. (**www.ojr.org/ojr/
law/1077150111.php**)

USC Annenberg Online
Journalism Review® — List of
companies offering Media Liability
Insurance (**www.ojr.org/ojr/
law/1077147945.php**)

Keywords

Amazon (**www.amazon.com/gp/
phrase/help/help.html**)

Google keyword tool (**https://
adwords.google.com/select/
KeywordToolExternal**)

Life Story Rights

Life story rights
(**www.absolutewrite.com/
screenwriting/life_rights.htm**)

Life story rights for movie
(**www.cfoyesq.com/forms_
life%20story%20rights%20
acquisition%20agreement.htm**)

Legal Information

Better Business Bureau's website
(**www.bbb.org**)

"Right of Publicity: an overview."
Legal Information Institute (LII).
Cornell University of Law.
(**http://topics.law.cornell.edu/
wex/publicity**)

State Attorney General
(**www.attorneygeneral.gov**)

Story rights and movie rights
(**http://listenusa.com/
WritersGuild.html**)

The Federal Trade Commission,
Bureau of Consumer Protection
(**www.ftc.gov**)

Volunteer Lawyers for the Arts
(**www.vlany.org**)

Literary Agents

AgentQuery (**www.agentquery. com**) — Agent Query offers a free searchable database of more than 900 literary agents.

Association of Author's Representatives (**www.aar-online. org**) — AAR is a professional organization for literary and dramatic agents. It was established in 1991 through the merger of the Society of Authors' Representatives, founded in 1928, and the Independent Literary Agents Association, founded in 1977. Browse its list of Member Agents.

Guide to Literary Agents (**www. guidetoliteraryagents.com**) — A Writer's Digest Book, this is a complete resource for writers who need representation.

Jeff Herman's Guide to Book Publishers, Editors, and Literary Agents (**www.jeffherman.com/guide**)

Preditors and Editors (**http://pred-ed.com/pubagent.htm**)

Publisher's Weekly (**www. publishersweekly.com**) — A weekly trade magazine targeting publishers, booksellers, literary agents, and libraries.

Publishers Marketplace (**www. publishersmarketplace.com**) — A resource for publishing professionals. A $20 subscription, payable monthly, gives you access to its articles and databases.

Query Shark (**http://queryshark.blogspot.com**)

Writer's Digest (**www.writersdigest.com**)

Writers Net (**www.writers.net/ agents.html**) — An Internet directory of writers, editors, publishers, and literary agents.

Logo Design

Guru Corporation's Logosnap.com. (**www.logosnap.com**)

HP's Logomaker (**www.logomaker.com**)

Marketing

eBook Market View (**http://ebmv.blogspot.com**)

eBook Newser (**www.mediabistro. com/ebooknewser**)

mocoNews.net (**http://moconews.net**)

News and Blogs

Author! Author! Anne Mini's Blog (**www.annemini.com/?cat=130**)

Entertainment Weekly: Books (**www.ew.com/ew/books**)

GalleyCat™. Mediabistro.com (**www.mediabistro.com/galleycat**)

Mashable (**http://mashable.com**)

Paste Magazine (**www.pastemagazine.com/ articles/books**)

Publishing Perspectives (**http:// publishingperspectives.com**)

Publishing.com (**www. pfspublishing.com**)

Silobreaker (**http://silobreaker.com**)

Teleread: News and views on e-books, libraries, publishing and related topics (**www.teleread.com**)

Writer Unboxed (**http://writerunboxed.com**)

Writing World (**www.writing-world.com**)

PDFs

Adobe (**www.adobe.com**)

Microsoft Word 2007 — Save as PDF or XPS (**www.microsoft. com/download/en/details. aspx?id=7**)

Recosoft (**www.recosoft.com**)

SolidDocuments (**www.soliddocuments.com**)

POD

Amazon's Create Space (**www.createspace.com**)

AuthorHouse (**www.authorhouse.com**)

iUniverse® (**www.iuniverse.com**)

LightningSource® (**www.lightningsource.com**)

Lulu (**www.lulu.com**)

Printers

Aeonix Publishing Group (**www.aeonix.com/bookprnt.htm**)

Bookmarket.com (**www.bookmarket.com/101print.htm**)

Independent Book Publishers' Association (**www.ibpa-online.org/vendors/suppliers.aspx**)

Literary Market Place (LMP) (**www.literarymarketplace.com**)

Morris Publishing (**www.morrispublishing.com**)

Small Publishers Association of North America (SPAN) (**www.spannet.org**)

NOOK Press

NOOK Press EPUB Formatting Guide (**https://www.nookpress.com/support**)

Research and Education

101 Best Websites for Writers — Writer's Digest (**www.writersdigest.com/101bestsites**)

Authors Market/Publish America (**www.authorsmarket.net/yourbook.htm**)

Free Tutorials Baycon Group (**www.baycongroup.com/el0.htm**)

Jeff Herman's Guide to Book Publishers, Editors, and Literary Agents (**www.jeffherman.com/guide**)

Publisher's Lunch (**www.publishersmarketplace.com**)

Publishers Weekly magazine online (**www.publishersweekly.com**)

The New York Times book reviews (**www.nytimes.com/pages/books**)

TitleZ – Amazon.com sales ranks (**www.titlez.com**)

Writer Beware® — Science Fiction and Fantasy Writers of America's Committee on Writing Scams (**www.sfwa.org/for-authors/writer-beware**)

Smashwords

Seven Secrets to E-book Publishing Success, Mark Coker (**www.slideshare.net/Smashwords/**

the-seven-secrets-of-ebook-publishing-success-7968488)

Smashwords Style Guide, by Smashwords founder Mark Coker (**www.smashwords.com/extreader/read/52/1/smashwords-style-guide**)

The Smashwords Book Marketing Guide, by Smashwords founder Mark Coker (**www.smashwords.com/extreader/read/305/1/smashwords-book-marketing-guide**)

Smashwords Satellites (**www.smashwords.com/labs**)

Social Media

Facebook (**www.facebook.com**)

LinkedIn (**www.linkedin.com**)

MySpace (**www.myspace.com**)

Twitter (**www.twitter.com**)

YouTube (**www.youtube.com**)

E-Commerce Website

2Checkout (**www.2checkout.com**)

Adobe Web analytics powered by Omniture (**www.omniture.com/en/products/online_analytics**)

Alexa (**www.alexa.com**)

ClickBank (**www.clickbank.com**)

Durango Merchant Services (**http://durangomerchantservices.com/**)

FastCharge (**www.fastcharge.com**)

Flagship Merchant Services (**www.flagshipmerchantservices.com**)

GoEmerchant (**www.goemerchant.com**)

Google Analytics (**www.google.com/support/analytics**)

Instamerchant (**www.instamerchant.com**)

Merchant Warehouse (**http://merchantwarehouse.com**)

Paypal (**www.paypal.com**)

Webtrends (**www.webtrends.com**)

HTML Basics

Common HTML Terms

HTML: Stands for HyperText Markup Language.

class attribute: An attribute whose value is common to an entire class of objects and not just to a value particular to each instance of the class.

attribute: A named property of a class that describes a data value held by each object in the class.

tag: Indicator used to set sections apart, such as bold text, italics, underlined text, and headings found within the <>. For example, a paragraph tag is "p," represented as <p>.

block-level element: A page element that defaults as a block on the page and will begin new line breaks around itself. Defaults to the width of the screen unless you add specifications for a certain width.

in-line element: Unlike the block-level element, the in-line element does not create new lines around itself. Bold <strong> and italics <em> fall into this category. In-line elements are contained within block-level elements.

CSS: Cascading Style Sheets. Styles are predesignated page elements that have a certain appearance, depending on how you designate the settings. CSS elements are organized in hierarchies.

HTML Basics

* Tag order is important. When more than one tag is written, it should appear like this:

Strong and emphasis equal bold and italic

* Make sure that you "end" your tags by including the / (see the example above). This is usually referred to as the open and close tag format.

* Two tags are stand-alone and do not require the forward slash closure. They are:

<HR> Horizontal Reference or Horizontal Rule: Gives you a horizontal line across the page.

 Break: a line break moves the text to the next line. Use in place of hitting "Enter."

* At the beginning of every page, designate the "doctype" such as:

<!DOCTYPE HTML PUBLIC "-//W3C//DTD HTML 4.01//EN"

"http://www.w3.org/TR/html4/strict.dtd">

This tells the browser which version of HTML you are using. If you use a Web design program, such as Dreamweaver®, this is inserted automatically into every document for you. If you use CSS (cascading style sheets), this header is particularly important. The exclamation mark at the beginning of the tag indicates a comment; comments are embedded within the page and do not display to the viewer.

Begin every page with <HTML> and end with </HTML>

The second tag on every page will always be <TITLE> and </TITLE>

Paragraph <p> and line break <br> tags are used to create new paragraphs and move the text to a new line, respectively, and do not need closing tags.

The following is a simple sample page:

```
<!--DOCTYPE HTML PUBLIC "-//W3C//DTD HTML 4.01//EN"
"http://www.w3.org/TR/html4/strict.dtd"-->
<html>
<head>
<title>A simple HTML document.</title>
</head>
<body>
<p>Part <strong>One</strong><p>
<br>
<p>The HTML Tutorial<p>
</body>
</html>
<!This is the end of the document>
```

- Use a plain text editor to write HTML, like Notepad, Simple Text, or WordPad. When you save the document, the default file extension is .txt. A plain text file saves the text only and does not convert or change it like a word processor would.

- If you use a word processor to write your HTML, the most important thing to remember is that every time you save your document, you must go to "File," choose "Save As," and save the document as Text or ASCII Text DOS on a PC or Text on a Mac. If you do not choose "Save As > Text," you will save your file as the default word processing document, which will interfere with your HTML.

- When you save your document, name it example.htm or example. html. Generally, use .htm if you are running on a system that uses Windows 3.x and .html on a Mac or for Windows 95/98 or later. This is important to tell your computer what type of file this is.

- Look at other documents similar to yours, especially when you are first learning HTML. When you find a document you like, look at its HTML code to see how it was done. To view a Web page's source code, right-click on it with your mouse and go to "View > Source."

- CSS takes care of elements that used to be handled by HTML, such as text size, which used to be designated with the <FONT SIZE> tag and is now handled with the style attribute, like this: <p style="font size: 150%;">This represents an in-line CSS style.</ p>

- CSS is written: Property: value; a property could be anything, such as the color, border, or font size, and the value is what you want the property to assume. These are separated with a colon and ended with a semi-colon to signify the completion of the property.

- w3schools.com offers a comprehensive reference for HTML tags (**www.w3schools.com/html/html_quick.asp**) and CSS attributes (**www.w3schools.com/cssref**).

Common HTML tags:

TAG	NAME	EXAMPLE
<!--	Comment	<!—Comments do not appear in the visible part of the document, only in the HTML-->
<a -	Anchor	<a href="http://www.amazon.com/">Visit Amazon</a>
<b>	Bold	<b>Text here will show as bold.</b>
<strong>	Bold	<strong>Text here will show as bold.</strong>
<i>	Italics	<i>Text here will show in italics.</i>
<em>	Italics	<em>Text here will show in italics.</em>
<big>	Big text	<big>Increases the size of the text. To increase the size of the text further, use two of this tag side by side.</big>
** **	Line break	This is the first line. This is the second line.
<body>	Body of document	<body>The entire contents of your Web page go between these tags.</body>
<center>	Center	<center>Everything between these tags will be centered.</center>
<dd>	Definition description	<dl> <dt>Definition Term</dt> <dd>Definition of the term.</dd> <dt>Definition Term</dt> <dd>Definition of the term.</dd> </dl>
<dt>	Definition term	See example above.
<dl>	Definition list	See <dd> example.
<font>	Font	<font face="Calibri" size="3" color="#003300">Sample text</font>
<head>	Document heading	<head>Elements here describe your HTML document, and are visible only in the HTML.</head>
<H1>	Heading 1	[Headings are commonly used for Web pages; browsers recognize headings as important page elements.] <H1>Heading 1 is the largest, about 24-point font.</H1>
<H2>	Heading 2	<H2>Heading 2 is the second largest, about 18-point font.</H2>
<H3>	Heading 3	<H3>Heading 3 is the third largest, about 13.5-point font.</H3>
<H4>	Heading 4	<H4>Heading 4 is the fourth largest, about 12-point font.</H4>
<H5>	Heading 5	<H5>Heading 5 is the fifth largest, about 10-point font.</H5>
<H6>	Heading 6	<H6>Heading 6 is the sixth largest, about 7.5 point font.</H6>

TAG	NAME	EXAMPLE
\<hr\>	Horizontal rule	\<p\>Web page contents\</p\> \<hr /\> \<p\>Web page contents\</p\>
\<img\>	Image	\<img src="FileOnYourComputer.gif" width="12" height="12" border="1" alt="text that describes image" /\>
\<li\>	List item	[Bullets can appear as a filled-in circle, open circle, or square:] \<menu\> \<li type="disc"\>List Item 1\</li\> \<li type="circle"\>List Item 2\</li\> \<li type="square"\>List Item 3\</li\> \</menu\>
\<link\>	Link	\<head\> \<link rel="stylesheet" type="text/css" href="style.css" /\>
\<menu\>	Menu	Menu tag precedes a list. See \<li\> example above.
\<meta\>	Meta	\<meta name="Description" content="Your site description here"\> \<meta name="keywords" content="Keywords describing site here"\>
\<ol\>	Ordered list	[Instead of bullets, list items can be listed by lower case roman numerals:] \<ol type="i"\> \<li\>List Item 1\</li\> \<li\>List Item 2\</li\> \<li\>List Item 3\</li\> \<li\>List Item 4\</li\> \</ol\>
\<p\>	Paragraph	\<p\>Creates both a line break and a space between lines: This is an example sentence.\<p\>This sentence is on the second line. \<p align="left"\>Use this tag to left-align the text that follows. \<p align="right"\>Use this tag to right-align the text that follows. \<p align="center"\>Use this tag to center the text that follows.
\<small\>	Small text	\<small\>Creates small text. Use two of these tags side by side to make the text even smaller.\</small\>
\<strike\>	Strikethrough	\<strike\>Strikes through this text.\</strike\>
\<title\>	Document title	\<title\>Title of the HTML page.\</title\>
\<u\>	Underline	\<u\>This text will be underlined.\</u\>

Sample Press Release and Review Query

Sample Press Release

FOR IMMEDIATE RELEASE

October 5, 2010

Children's Book Reveals the Importance of Team Sports

New York, N.Y. — Bestselling children's author Jane Writer explores the other side of youth sports in her latest book from Best Books Ever, *Jiminy Jumping Jacks!* Released in October 2010, *Jiminy Jumping Jacks!* is available for $4.95 as an e-book from Barnes & Noble Booksellers, Amazon.com, and e-book retailers.

Writer's picture book promises to make an impact on children everywhere who struggle with weight problems. These children often suffer from low self-esteem and feelings of inadequacy, especially when it comes to participating in team sports. While the situation may be grim for a portion of American's population, Writer makes a bleak situation fun and addresses a difficult topic effortlessly. The story of turtle and his friends exhibits a supportive situation that is sure to be a hit with parents, teachers, and children's librarians.

Writer has taught physical education to children for 10 years, and has seen firsthand the positive effects of team sports on overweight children. Her program, "Fitness is Fun," has helped more than 75 children reduce their weight and see measurable health benefits. And Writer certainly has an audience — according to a recent study, one out of every three American children is overweight or obese. Says Writer, "Educating children about eating right and the importance of exercise is vital. But children don't have to know that — I hope my book makes it fun for them."

For additional information, contact Netty Networker at (555) 555-1234.

About Jane Writer: The award-winning author of *This is My Bus, Jimmy's Magic Day,* and *The Dog that Wouldn't Stop Running,* Jane Writer is a dedicated and talented writer for children. She has published stories in *Highlights for Children, American Girl, Muse, Cricket,* and *Nick.* When she isn't writing or reading to kids, she loves to go horseback riding and take picnic lunches with her three children.

CONTACT INFORMATION:
Netty Networker
XYZ PR Firm, Inc.
(555) 555-1234 (voice)
(555) 555-2345 (fax)
netty@xyzpr.com
www.xyzpr.com

Sample Review Query (Email)

Email address: Ricky Reviewer at Publication of the Month

Subject: Review query for *Jiminy Jumping Jacks!*

My book recently was released from Best Books Ever. I am writing to ask if you would be interested in reviewing it. *Jiminy Jumping Jacks!* is the tale of a young turtle's struggle to live up to the athletic triumphs of his best friends, Rabbit and Fox.

With an increasing focus on keeping kids healthy, parents, teachers, and librarians will appreciate the values represented in the adventures of the three friends. The book is fun for kids to read, and not only shows the importance of eating right and exercise, but also deals with an experience many kids can relate to. For children whose athletic abilities are not quite at the level as those of their friends, participating in sports can be disheartening. Children who are overweight often struggle with body image and feelings of social inadequacy, and turtle's interactions with his friends are taken from real-life examples.

I have taught physical education for 10 years and have seen firsthand the effects that feeling inadequate has on children's self-esteem. Not many children's books address this topic, and I hope that mine call fill a void while showing children that they can turn this difficult situation around through both perseverance *and* fun.

Please let me know if you are interested, and I will gladly send a complimentary e-book. Thank you for your time.

Thank you!

Jane Writer
1234 Show-Don't-Tell Lane
Boston, MA 02101

January 1, 20--

Sample Review Slip

Best Books Ever Presents for Review

Title: *The Legacy of Thomas Edison: More than Just the Inventor of the Light Bulb*

Author: Cynthia Reeser

Edition: First

Number in Print: 100,000

CIP/LCCN: 1234567890

ISBN: 1-23456-789-0

Pages: 64

Cover art: Illustration by Cynthia Reeser

Price: $14.95

Season: Fall 2010

Publication date: October 2010

Rights:

    a. Subsidiary: Book club, paperback

    b. Syndication

Please email a copy of your review to **Info@BestBooksEver.com**

Best Books Ever

1234 Bindery Blvd.

New York City, NY 10010

Tel: (555) 555-1234; Fax: (555) 555-2345

Info@BestBooksEver.com

www.BestBooksEver.com

Bibliography

"AAP Publishers Report Strong Growth in Year-to-Year, Year-End Book Sales." Association of American Publishers. February 16, 2011. (**http://www.publishers.org/press/24**)

"Amazon Kindle e-book downloads outsell paperbacks." BBC News Business. January 28, 2011. (**ww.bbc.co.uk/news/business-12305015**)

"Are E-Readers Greener Than Books?" *The New York Times.* August 31, 2009. (**http://green.blogs.nytimes.com/2009/08/31/are-e-readers-greener-than-books**)

Bosman, Julie and Jeremy W. Peters. "In E-Books, Publishers Have Rivals: News Sites." *The New York Times*, September 18, 2011. (**www.nytimes.com/2011/09/19/business/media/in-e-books-publishing-houses-have-a-rival-in-news-sites.html?_r=1&pagewanted=all**)

Bosman, Julie. "E-Book Author Signs Print Deal With Simon & Schuster." *The New York Times, Arts Beat.* August 22, 2011. (**http://artsbeat.blogs.nytimes.com/2011/08/22/e-book-author-signs-print-deal-with-simon-schuster**)

Buchanan, Matt. "Giz Explains: How You're Gonna Get Screwed By Ebook Formats." *Gizmodo.com*. March 10, 2010. (**http://gizmodo.com/5478842/giz-explains-how-youre-gonna-get-screwed-by-ebook-formats**)

Coker, Mark. *Smashwords Style Guide*. May 5, 2008. (**www.smashwords.com/books/view/52**)

Dubner, Stepehn J. "What Is Stephen King Trying to Prove?" *The New York Times Magazine*. August 13, 2000. (**http://partners. nytimes.com/library/magazine/home/20000813mag-king. html?scp=10&sq=riding%20the%20bullet&st=cse**)

Duell, Mark. "Thriller writer becomes first self-published author to sell one MILLION Kindle e-books… (then writes a eBook all about it!) *The Daily Mail*. Mail Online. June 22, 2011. (**www.dailymail.co.uk/news/ article-2006629/John-Locke-sells-1-million-Kindle-eBooks.html**)

"eBook Discovery and Sampling Skyrocketing at Public Libraries." OverDrive press release. Dallas, Texas. January 19, 2012 (**www.overdrive.com/News/eBook-Discovery-and-Sampling-Skyrocketing-at-Public-Libraries**)

Ferguson, Kevin. "For Softlock, the Rights Stuff Wasn't Good Enough." *Bloomberg Business Week*. December 26, 2000. (**www.businessweek.com/ebiz/0012/ec1226.htm**)

Fulton, Scott M., III. "How Deep is Amazon's Love for HTML5 in Kindle Format 8?" ReadWrite Hack. October 27, 2011. (**www.readwriteweb.com/hack/2011/10/how-deep-is-amazons-love-for-h.php**)

How Green are E-Books? *Living On Earth*. Air Date: Week of February 25, 2011. (**www.loe.org/shows/segments.html?programID=11-P13-00008&segmentID=5**)

Lebert, Marie. "eBooks: 1998 — The first ebook readers." *Project Gutenberg News.* July 16, 2011. (**www.gutenbergnews.org/20110716/ ebooks-1998-the-first-ebook-readers**)

Magee, David. "John Locke Author: Secrets to Self-Publishing Success." *The Daily Mail.* September 3, 2011. (**www.ibtimes.com/ articles/208153/20110903/john-locke-author-secrets-self-publishing-success-amazon-kindle-donovan-creed-simon-schuster.htm**)

Memmott, Carol. "Authors catch fire with self-published e-books." *USA Today.* February 9, 2011. (**www.usatoday.com/life/books/news/2011-02-09-ebooks09_ST_N.htm**)

Memmott, Carol. "Jaycee Dugard's memoir breaking sales records." Book Buzz. *USA Today.* July 13, 2011. (**http://books.usatoday.com/ bookbuzz/post/2011/07/jaycee-dugards-memoir-breaking-sales-records/176830/1**)

Miller, Sarah. "How a failed author made $2 million from e-books." *Toronto Star. thestar.com.* March 3, 2011. (**www.thestar.com/ entertainment/books/article/948078--how-a-failed-author-made-2-million-from-e-books**)

Mundahl, Hans. "So You Want to Use Digital Textbooks Next Year?" Ed Social Media. April 1, 2011. (**www.edsocialmedia.com/2011/04/so-you-want-to-use-e-textbooks-next-year**)

Nawotka, Edward. "New US Lawsuit Accuses Apple of E-Book Price Fixing." Publishing Perspectives. August 9, 2011. (**http:// publishingperspectives.com/2011/08/lawsuit-accuses-apple-of-price-fixing-attacks-agency-model**)

Purcell, Kristen. "E-reader Ownership Doubles in Six Months, Tablet Adoption Grows More Slowly." Pew Internet Project. June 27, 2011.

(http://pewresearch.org/pubs/2039/e-reader-ownership-doubles-tablet-adoption-grows-more-slowly)

Redden, Elizabeth. "Toward an All E-Textbook Campus." Inside Higher Ed. January 14, 2009. (www.insidehighered.com/news/2009/01/14/ebooks#ixzz1bVu292VC)

Rinzler, Alan. "Advice for Amanda Hocking from authors and agents." *Forbes.* April 4, 2011. (www.forbes.com/sites/booked/2011/04/04/advice-for-amanda-hocking-from-authors-and-agents)

Rowinski, Dan. "Kindle E-Books Now Outselling All Paper Books on Amazon." ReadWriteWeb. May 19, 2011. (www.readwriteweb.com/archives/kindle_e-books_now_outselling_all_paper_books_on_a.php)

Rusch, Kristine Kathryn. "The Business Rusch: How Traditional Publishers Are Making Money." November 16, 2011. (http://kriswrites.com/2011/11/16/the-business-rusch-how-traditional-publishers-are-making-money)

Saroyan, Strawberry. "Storyseller." *The New York Times Magazine.* June 17, 2011. (www.nytimes.com/2011/06/19/magazine/amanda-hocking-storyseller.html?pagewanted=1&_r=1)

Silverman, Julia. "Readers' Choice: Books vs. E-books." *Green Dilemmas.* Pamplin Media Group. August 18, 2011. (http://portlandtribune.com/sustainable/story.php?story_id=131343716079514100)

Sporkin, Andi. "Popularity of Books in Digital Platforms Continues to Grow, According to AAP Publishers February 2011 Sales Report." Association of American Publishers. April 14, 2011. (www.publishers.org/press/30)

Woudstra, Wendy J. "What is Libel?" PUBLISHING Central. (http://publishingcentral.com/articles/20030119-1-1d84.html?si=1)

Author Biography

Martha Maeda is a freelance writer, ghostwriter, and author of more than 20 books including *The Complete Guide to Green Building and Remodeling Your Home, Basic Guide to Investing in ETFs, How to Wipe Out Student Loans, How to Solar Power Your Home, How to Open & Operate a Financially Successful Independent Record Label,* and *101 Sunday School Activities on a Tiny Budget.* She enjoys helping people who might not otherwise become authors to self-publish their work and discover their writing potential. She currently lives with her family in Orlando, Florida.

Index